D&S VOL. 49 — REVISED EDITION!

F6F HELLCAT

in detail & scale

Bert Kinzey

squadron/signal publications

COPYRIGHT © 1996 BY DETAIL & SCALE, INC.

All rights reserved. No part of this publication may be reproduced in any form, stored in a retrieval system, or transmitted by any means, electronic, mechanical, or otherwise, except in a review, without the written consent of the publisher.

This book is a product of Detail & Scale, Inc., which has sole responsibility for its content and layout, except that all contributors are responsible for the security clearance and copyright release of all materials submitted. Published by Squadron/Signal Publications, 1115 Crowley Drive, Carrollton, Texas 75011. ISBN 1-888974-00-1

CONTRIBUTORS AND SOURCES:

Dana Bell
Jim Roeder

Dave Pluth
Stan Piet

Don Harris
Warren Munkasy

Captain David McCampbell, USN (Retired)
National Museum of Naval Aviation
National Air & Space Museum
Grumman Aerospace History Center
U. S. Marine Corps Air & Land Museum
Yanks Air Museum, Chino, California
Planes of Fame Museum, Chino, California

A special thanks is due to Lois Lovisolo of the Grumman History Center. Her efforts, cooperation, and patience were instrumental in the preparation of this book. Unfortunately, Grumman Aerospace has eliminated this outstanding reference center since this book was first released in 1987.

Another special thanks is also due to Captain Robert Rasmussen, USN (Ret.), Bill Johnson, Hill Goodspeed, and the volunteers at the National Museum of Naval Aviation.

Detail & Scale and the author extend thanks to Mike Starn of the U. S. Marine Corps Air & Land Museum at Quantico, Virginia, for his time and assistance.

Many photographs in this publication are credited to their contributors. Photographs with no credit indicated were taken by the author.

Left (Front cover): This illustration by Don Greer depicts an F6F-5 Hellcat from VF-9 as it appeared in February 1945. At that time, VF-9 was embarked aboard the USS LEXINGTON (CV-16).

Right (Rear cover): Details and colors of the instrument panel in an F6F-3 can be studied in this large photograph. Note that what at first may appear to be a center console is not really attached to the instrument panel. Instead, it is a separate pedestal which is located under and a few inches forward of the main instrument panel.

INTRODUCTION

This head-on view of an F6F-3 reveals many details of the large, radial-engined Hellcat. Note the dihedral of the wings from the center sections outward, the stance on the landing gear, the .50 caliber machine guns, and the pitot tube under the right wing tip. The flaps are up, but the ailerons are deflected, showing the aileron under the right wing behind the national insignia.   (Grumman)

Because the format of the Detail & Scale Series requires a considerable number of detailed photographs of the featured aircraft, it has been particularly difficult to do books on World War II subjects. While it is relatively easy to gain access to present-day aircraft and take the many specific and detailed photographs that are required, obtaining such photographs of subjects which are no longer operational is far more difficult.

In 1987, The F6F Hellcat in Detail & Scale, became the first book in the Detail & Scale Series to feature a World War II fighter. This was followed in 1988 by The F4F Wildcat in Detail & Scale. Both of these titles were made possible because the Grumman History Center had maintained extensive files of detailed photographs for most of the aircraft the company had produced. Likewise, the titles on the B-17 and B-29 were made possible because Boeing had maintained similar photo files.

Although using photographs available from the manufacturer made these books on World War II aircraft possible, it still was not as effective as being able to go out and take exactly the desired photographs. But the fiftieth anniversary of World War II has changed this situation to a considerable extent. The renewed interest in World War II aircraft has lead to two very important changes in the availability and accuracy of the aircraft of that era that remain today. Over the past few years, a number of aircraft have been recovered from Lake Michigan and elsewhere. Others that were lying derelict in pastures or even in the back lots of cities have been rediscovered. Once found and reclaimed, these aircraft have been, and continue to be, restored with a much greater emphasis on accuracy than ever before. While these restorations usually do not produce an aircraft that meets every factory specification, they do provide a very good resource for studying and illustrating what the military aircraft of over fifty years ago looked like. In many cases, every detail possible is reproduced with care, and all paint colors are matched as closely as possible to the original.

When this book was originally released, there were no restored F6F-3 Hellcats. Today, there is one at the National Museum of Naval Aviation in Pensacola, Florida, another at the Marine Corps Museum at Quantico, Virginia, and a third at the National Air and Space Museum's restoration facility at Silver Hill, Maryland. During the revision of this book, all three of these aircraft were visited and photographed extensively. Several more F6F-5s have been restored as well. One of these is at the Yanks Air Museum in Chino, California, and another is at the Planes of Fame Museum, also at Chino. Both of these were photographed for this revised edition.

In revising The F6F Hellcat in Detail & Scale, all seven pages of Hellcat details (pages 8 through 14) have been completely redone. Over thirty new detailed photographs have been added to this section of the book, and these were taken specifically for this publication.

There are two new pages of color as well. A detailed look at the cockpit in an F6F-3 is on page 38, while six color photographs of the Pratt & Whitney R2800 engine are shown on page 40. All of these new photographs, both color and black and white, illustrate the Hellcat in more detail than ever before. They will be very helpful to the scale modeler in building the latest Hellcat kits.

Other important features remain the same. The five-view scale drawings by Dana Bell were done from the official Grumman factory drawings of the Hellcat which were thought lost for many years. They remain the most accurate drawings of the Hellcat ever published. Also included again is the interview with Captain David McCampbell, USN (Retired), the Navy's all-time leading ace. It contains information and photographs about him and the Hellcat that have never been published elsewhere.

The Modelers Section has been updated to include the new Hellcat kits that have become available since the first release of this book. These include the Minicraft 1/72nd scale kit and the 1/48th scale kits from Hasegawa. Revised releases of older kits are also covered.

By combining the best of the original edition with the new revisions, The F6F Hellcat in Detail & Scale remains the most detailed book about the Navy's most important fighter of World War II ever published.

HISTORICAL SUMMARY

The XF6F-1 is shown here in overall bare metal. More details of the XF6F-1 are shown on page 16.   (Grumman)

There are many ways to judge a fighter aircraft. Often its speed and maneuverability are measured to ascertain how good it is. But is fighter A better than fighter B just because it is faster, or is fighter C better than fighter D because it is more maneuverable? If so, why didn't the Japanese Zeke annihilate every fighter it faced? Sometimes other yardsticks are used, but many factors go in to what makes a given aircraft an outstanding fighter. What is the real purpose of a fighter aircraft? A fighter is designed primarily to shoot down the enemy's aircraft in air-to-air combat and gain air superiority. A fighter should be judged on how well it accomplishes this purpose. If this criterion alone is used, a strong argument could be made that the Hellcat was the greatest fighter of all time. In only two years of combat, Hellcats shot down 5156 enemy aircraft in air-to-air combat. This is the most aerial victories ever scored by one type of fighter. Many more enemy aircraft were destroyed on the ground. The breakdown of air-to-air kills was as follows: Carrier-based F6Fs shot down 4947 enemy aircraft, while an additional 209 were shot down by land-based Navy and Marine units. Of the 6477 kills scored by Navy and Marine pilots, three out of every four were made in the Hellcat. Only 270 F6Fs were lost in combat, resulting in a 19 to 1 kill ratio.

All of this is not to say that the Hellcat was the best fighter of all time or even of World War II. It never had to fight other American fighters, nor did it have to fight British or even German fighters on a large scale. It was designed to defeat Japanese fighters, and at this it was very successful. It would be impossible to pick any fighter as undeniably the best of all time, but the Hellcat certainly performed its mission as well as any fighter ever produced.

The XF6F-1 began as Grumman's Design Number 50. A contract was placed for two prototypes, 02981 and 02982, on June 30, 1941. The first of these made its maiden flight on June 26, 1942, flown by test pilot Robert L. Hall. This Hellcat was originally powered by a Wright R2600-16 engine that turned a Curtiss Electric three-bladed prop and produced 1600 horsepower. But this was quickly changed to a Pratt & Whitney R2800-10 and a Hamilton Standard propeller that produced 2000 horsepower. As has often been the case with Grumman's aircraft, there was very little change in the design of the 12,200 Hellcats produced over the years. In fact, the Hellcat was the least modified of any fighter that served for any amount of time in World War II. This is a testimony to what was an excellent design in the first place, and a tribute to the designers, engineers, and work force at Grumman.

Grumman's design philosophy can be contrasted to

Grumman produced the Hellcat in large quantities very quickly. Here fuselages of F6F-3s are shown on the assembly line at the Grumman plant in Bethpage, New York.   (Grumman)

With flaps down and engine racing, a Hellcat does final checks just prior to launch. When the Hellcat entered service, most launches were accomplished simply by flying the aircraft off the flight deck. But the catapults were used more and more in the later stages of the war. Noteworthy are the fairings over the .50 caliber machine guns. These fairings were installed on approximately the first 900 F6F-3s built. (U.S. Navy via Grumman)

that of Vought's, who produced another excellent fighter in World War II, the F4U Corsair. Grumman stuck with a simple, straight-forward design that was easily mass-produced, and was also reliable. Many of the lines of the previous F4F Wildcat were used in the Hellcat. Therefore, Grumman's design was a known quantity for the most part, while Vought was involved with the more radical. While the Corsair proved itself to be a superb fighter in the air, its unorthodox design proved unsatisfactory for carrier operations until modifications could be made. Later, Vought had similar problems with its F7U Cutlass and F8U Crusader. Both had radical design features when compared to their contemporaries. The F7U had a design like no other aircraft in the air, and featured twin tails and a long nose landing gear strut that was both troublesome and dangerous for carrier operations. The F8U had a never-before-tried variable incidence wing. Its centerline and thrust line were virtually the same, and this resulted in some unusual flight characteristics, particularly when power was quickly applied. Both were great aircraft in the air, but had their problems operating on carriers.

It is not the purpose here to argue which company followed the best course, because both had merits. But it could be said that Grumman had less problems. While the Corsair would remain in front line service for a longer period of time once the problems were solved, Grumman's approach was to build it simple, build it rugged, and build, build, build! At one point, in March 1945, Grumman produced 605 Hellcats in a month's time, and the Navy asked for a slow down in time of war!

One of the problems that was encountered with producing the Hellcat was the lack of plant space at Bethpage. Grumman obtained steel from the disassembled Second Avenue elevated railway in New York City to help build Plant 3. It has been reported that some of this steel went into the production of the Hellcats, but the fact is

This photograph has the words "O'Hare's Favorite" written on the back, making reference to the Medal of Honor winner, Butch O'Hare. Over two hundred bullet holes were counted in the skin of this F6F-3. The Hellcat was a very rugged aircraft, and was able to absorb a great deal of punishment. Note the nine victory flags under the cockpit which indicate that this Hellcat did its share of dishing out punishment as well as taking it.

(Grumman)

Grumman employees gather around the "Hirohito Special," which was the 10,000th Hellcat built. (Grumman)

that it was for the building, not for the aircraft! The plant opened on June 1, 1942, still not completed.

Incorporated into the Hellcat's design was a 250 gallon internal fuel tank that provided it with the range that the Wildcat lacked. A distinctively shaped external tank of 150 gallons could be carried on the centerline, and two more smaller tanks could be fitted to pylons under the center section of the wings. However, these were seldom used. Armament consisted of six .50 caliber guns on most Hellcats, but 20mm cannon were mixed in on F6F-5N night fighters. Up to 400 rounds per gun could be carried. Both the -3 and -5 could carry up to 1000-pound bombs, and six five-inch rockets could be carried by the -5.

Since the victor in air-to-air combat was often the one who saw the other first, the Hellcat was designed with good visibility. The cowl line from the cockpit forward sloped slightly downward, and the pilot sat high in the cockpit. Survivability was important, both for the plane and the pilot. Grumman's "Iron Works" produced planes of steel that performed like sterling, and considerable protection was provided for the pilot. The Hellcat did not explode or catch fire when hit like the Japanese aircraft were prone to do. It was easy to fly, even coming aboard a carrier, and this was due in a large part to the largest wing on any single-engine U.S. fighter in World War II.

The XF6F-2 was an experimental aircraft to test the addition of a turbo-supercharger, but these tests did not prove successful enough to justify the production of the F6F-2. Thus, the first production version of the Hellcat was the F6F-3, and, as photographs on the following pages illustrate, there was little change from the original design of the XF6F-1. The first flight of an F6F-3 was made in October 1942, and the first production aircraft was 04775. A total of 4402 F6F-3s were built, with production changing to the F6F-5 in April 1944. The Royal Navy's Fleet Air Arm received 252 F6F-3s, which were originally called Gannets by the British, but later the name was changed to Hellcat I.

There were three sub-variants of the F6F-3. One was a photographic version that was made by simply adding cameras to the basic F6F-3. Most carriers had from two to four of these F6F-3Ps included in their squadrons to record the effects of strikes against land and sea targets.

The other two sub-variants were night fighters. The F6F-3E, of which only eighteen were built, had an AN/APS-4 radar in a pod under its right wing. The more numerous F6F-3N (approximately 200 built) had an AN/APS-6 radar in a fairing on the leading edge of its right wing. Details of these two versions of the Hellcat night fighters may be seen beginning on page 28.

Carrier qualifications began on the USS ESSEX, CV-9, in February 1943. The combat debut was on August 31, 1943, with Hellcats from ESSEX, YORKTOWN (CV-10), and INDEPENDENCE (CVL-22), making a raid against Marcus Island. Thus, only fourteen months had elapsed between the time the prototype made its first flight until the Hellcat entered combat. The strike was led by CDR Jimmy Flatley who was flying an F6F-3 with three external tanks so that he could stay over the target and direct strikes for the longest possible period of time. The strike was very successful, and although no enemy aircraft got into the air, several were destroyed on the ground during the Hellcat's baptism of fire. Only two Hellcats and one Avenger were lost to anti-aircraft fire, while a third Hellcat had to ditch. The pilot of the ditching Hellcat and the crew of the Avenger were rescued.

While producing the F6F-3, Grumman took the original XF6F-1 and modified it to carry four 20mm cannons instead of the usual six .50 caliber machine guns. This was designated the XF6F-4 (see page 32), but it was not placed in production. The F6F-5 then became the second and most extensively produced version of the Hellcat. A total of 7870 F6F-5s were built, with 930 going to England as Hellcat IIs.

There was little change in design from the F6F-3, but it was easy to tell the F6F-5 from the -3 because of its overall glossy sea blue finish that replaced the three-color

As the war progressed, fighters made up a larger and larger percentage of the complement of aircraft on the carriers. Therefore, in addition to air-to-air combat, they also had to be used to attack surface targets on the land and sea. Rocket racks were a permanent installation beginning on late F6F-3s and on the F6F-5. Bombs could also be carried. Here a Hellcat flies over a Japanese destroyer during the attack on Truk in February 1944.

(International News Photo via Grumman)

Outside the plant at Bethpage, Hellcats share the parking area with the two Grumman piston-driven fighters that followed it into production. An F8F Bearcat can be seen at the center of the photo, and a twin engine F7F Tigercat is visible near the building just to the right of center. (Grumman)

scheme of the F6F-3. The R2800-10W engine with water injection, that had been installed in the last F6F-3s, provided the power. Armament remained six .50 caliber machine guns. The big improvement was the ability of the -5 to serve as a fighter-bomber, and provisions for carrying six five-inch rockets under the wings were standard. Bombs could be carried under the wing center section. Spring tabs were added to the ailerons to reduce control forces, and this proved helpful in air-to-air combat. At slow speeds the Zeke was still more maneuverable, but at high speeds the Hellcat was a good match. It was faster than the Zeke at all altitudes, and could outclimb it above 10,000 feet. The aft section of the fuselage and tail was strengthened, and the cowl was tighter fitting. The first -5s had the rear windows behind the cockpit, but these were soon deleted.

The F6F-5 first flew in April 1944, and quickly thereafter was replacing the -3 in squadrons. Production began in that month, and continued until November 16, 1945, when the Navy accepted the last F6F-5. As with the -3, there was a photographic F6F-5P that was made simply by adding cameras to the basic F6F-5 airframe. F6F-5E and F6F-5N night fighters were built by adding the AN/APS-4 and AN/APS-6 radars respectively to the F6F-5. The F6F-5N was fitted with a mixed battery of two 20mm cannon and four .50 caliber machine guns. Coverage of the F6F-5 begins on page 45, with details of the night fighters beginning on page 49.

Had the war continued, the XF6F-6 would have been the next production version of the Hellcat, but this never came to pass. Other versions of the Hellcat were also proposed, to include one with a bigger wing, and another with a combination of piston and jet powerplants like what actually flew in the form of the Ryan Fireball. But none of these ever got past the drawing stage.

After the war, Hellcats were provided to France and Urugray. They remained in service with the U.S. Navy in reserve and training units into the early 1950s. They were also used as drones, and a few were used as flying drone bombs during the war in Korea. But they rather quickly disappeared from first line units as the F8F Bearcat, later versions of the F4U Corsair, and then the new jets replaced them. But by then the Hellcat had done the job it was designed for, that of winning the air war against Japan, and had done probably better than even its designers had ever imagined.

On the pages that follow is a detailed look at the prototypes and the versions of the Hellcat that were produced. Details common to most or all versions are illustrated first. A look at each type begins with the XF6F-1 on page 16.

The Hellcat was the first Navy fighter to be fitted operationally with a radar for use in the night fighter role. Here an F6F-5N flies in formation with two of its successors. A night fighter version of the Corsair and a Skyknight are also shown in this photograph. (National Archives)

HELLCAT DETAILS
MAIN LANDING GEAR

The right main landing gear is shown here from the outside. The wheel is the earlier style used on Hellcats, however it could be found on Hellcats throughout their service life.

This front view provides a look at the oleo scissors and the small gear door at the top of the strut. Note the small notch in the door at the top on the inboard side.

Details of the interior of the right main gear well can be seen in this view that looks forward. The large hook in the center of the well locked the strut in the "up" position when the gear was retracted.

The aft end of the gear well is shown here. The photograph looks up and aft into the well, and the separation between the inner and outer flaps can be seen at the bottom of the photo. Note that the line of separation for the wing fold runs right through this portion of the gear well.

The main gear door was attached to the strut and rotated with it as the gear retracted. This is the left main gear as seen from the front right. Note the catapult bridle attached to the hook just inboard of the gear.

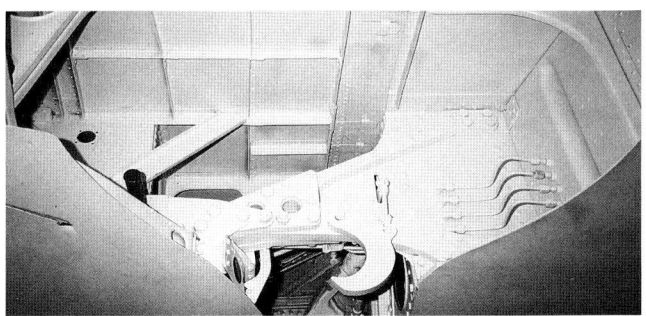

The wheel and tire were housed in the large, round, aft portion of the well when retracted. This is the forward end of that area in the left gear well.

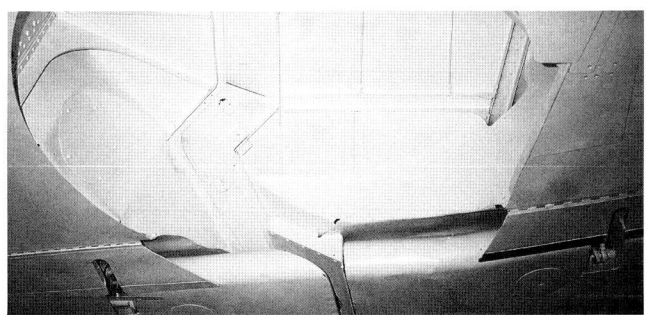

This is the aft end of the left wheel well where it meets the flaps. Note the wedge-shaped part of the wheel well structure between the inner and outer flaps.

The later style main gear wheel is shown here. However, photographs of Hellcats in service reveal that this style of wheel was used on F6F-3s and F6F-5s alike.

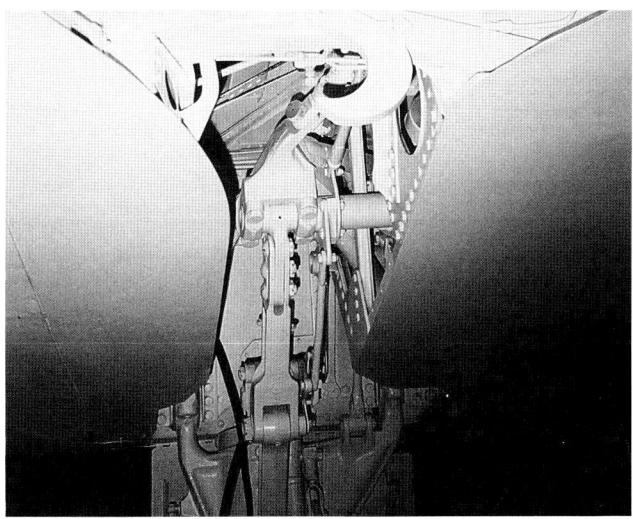

This view looks forward in the left main gear well. Part of the retraction mechanism is visible.

TAIL WHEEL & ARRESTING HOOK

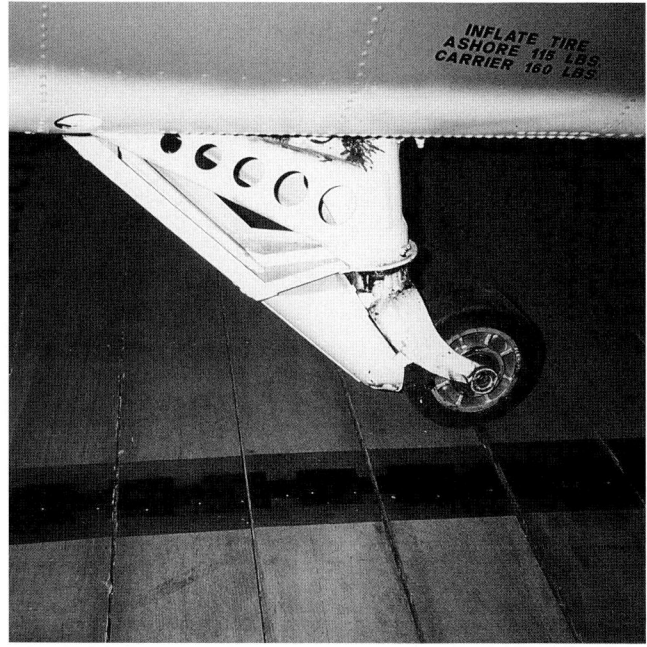

Above left: A pneumatic tail wheel tire was developed for the Hellcat, and it was used on F6Fs based on land and on carriers. It was a 10 X 4 Goodrich Silvertown tire. Inflation was 115 psi for land use and 160 psi for carrier operations.   (Grumman)

Above right: A hard rubber tire was more common aboard ship. Details of the Hellcat's solid rubber tail wheel tire can be seen here. The tail wheel was a retractable unit. It is interesting to see the inflation information stencilled on the aircraft even though the hard rubber tire is installed on this aircraft.

Left: The tail wheel assembly is seen here from the front right. The door was attached to the front of the strut, and it was curved to match the contours of the underside of the fuselage.

The arresting hook was housed completely inside the tail cone as shown in the photograph at left. At right is a look at the extended arresting hook. Note the small white position light just above the retracted arresting hook in the photograph at left.
(Both Grumman)

WING FOLD DETAILS

The photographs on this page show the wing fold details on the left wing. The right wing was simply a mirror image of what is illustrated here. This photo shows the wing fold joint and hinge at the leading edge of the wing.

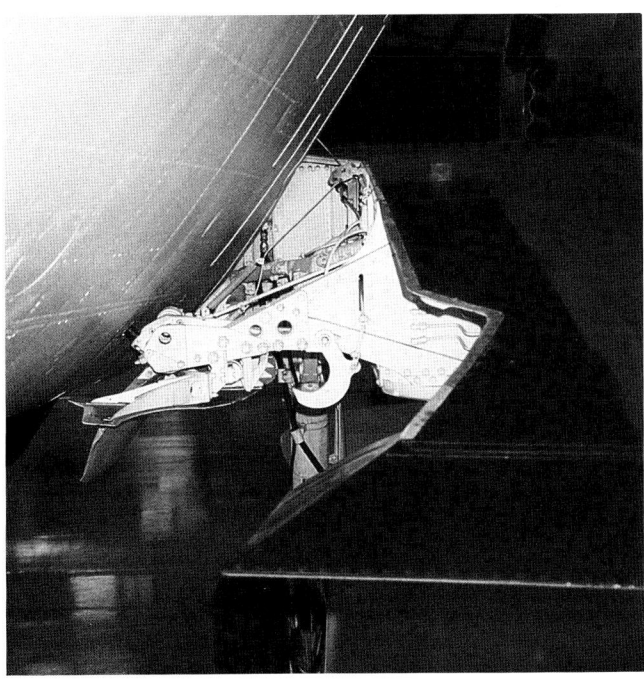

The fact that the wing fold was through the main gear well can be seen in this photo taken from the trailing edge of the wing.

When the wings were folded, a small red cylinder popped up on the top of the wing. It can be seen here between the wing fold and the non-skid walkway.

Details of the outer wing panel at the fold line are shown here. This area was usually painted the same color as the underside of the wing.

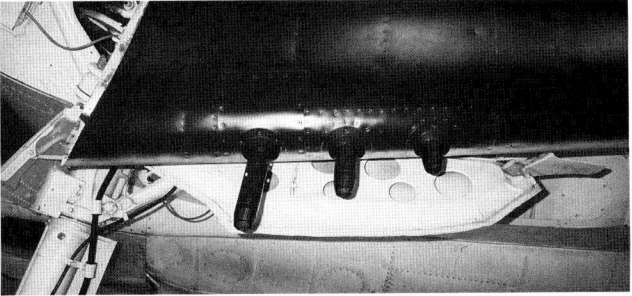

A panel on the underside of the wing hinged down as the wing folded. It can be seen behind the guns in this view.

The cylinder dropped down flush with the top of the wing when the wing was locked into the extended position. The pilot checked both cylinders to make sure they were in this position before taking off in the aircraft.

WING DETAILS

The gun camera was located in the wing root of the left wing. Access to the camera was through the hinged panel directly above the camera installation.

Also located on the leading edge of the left wing was the landing and taxi light. It was mounted just outboard of the guns. Note how the lens of the light is parallel to the ground rather than to the dihedral of the wing. The first 272 F6F-3s had the retractable light under the left wing as seen in the top photo on page 5, but all subsequent aircraft had the light as shown here.

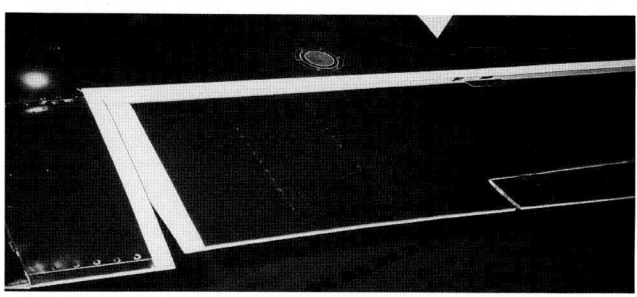

A small, circular, blue light was installed on the top of each wing just forward of the aileron.

Navigation lights were located on the tip of each wing at the leading edge. The lens for each light was clear, while the bulb inside was red on the left wing and green on the right wing.

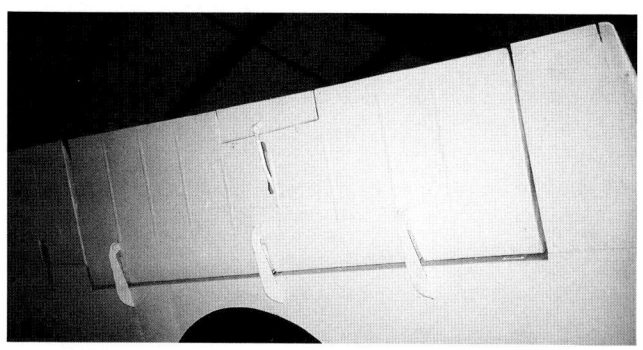

This underside view of the right aileron shows the three large hinges and the trim tab. Note the actuator for the trim tab.

A retractable catapult bridle hook was mounted under each wing just inboard of the main landing gear.

A non-skid walkway was applied to the top of each wing at the root. The shape and size of this walkway varied from aircraft to aircraft.

FUSELAGE DETAILS

Two lights were located on the spine of the aircraft. The front light was white, and the aft light was green. A whip antenna as usually installed just behind the rear light as shown here.

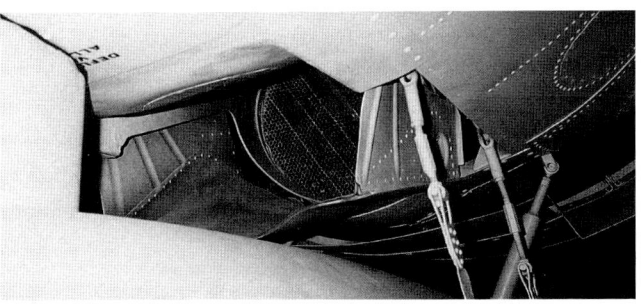

A hinged vent door was located just aft of the oil cooler. This view looks up and forward into the door from the right. The rear of the cooler can be seen inside the door.

Another whip antenna was usually on the underside of the fuselage. However, the number and location of the whip antennas varied depending on the radio equipment that was installed in the aircraft.

These two photographs show the lower exhausts and the cooling flaps at the aft end of the engine accessory compartment. Note the valves for the fuel strainers inside each flap. It should be noted that the arm that moves the flap in the right photo has been removed. This allows for the flap to be opened further, and it provides an unobstructed view of the valve inside the flap.

TAIL DETAILS

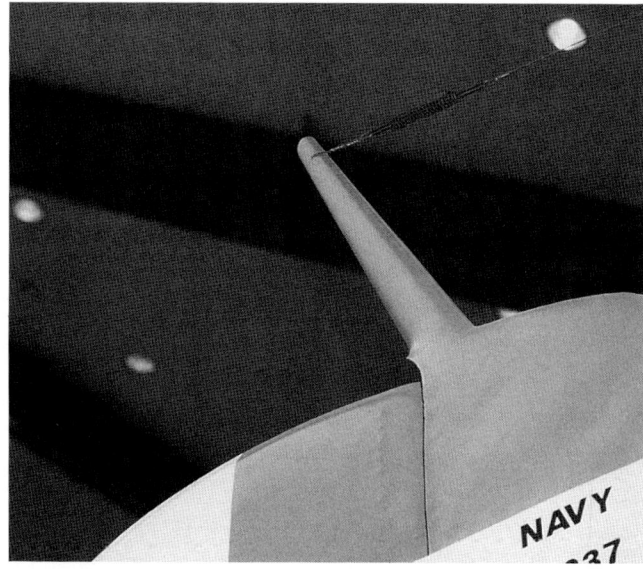

Above: The radio antenna wire was attached to a mast mounted at an angle on the tip of the vertical tail. Although the front mast angled forward on early F6F-3s and was vertical on late F6F-3s and the F6F-5, this aft mast was angled rearward on all variants.

Right: Here is an overall view of the left side of the tail on an F6F-5. Note that the rudder was covered with fabric.

The top of the left horizontal stabilizer and elevator can be seen here. The elevators were covered with fabric.

The right horizontal stabilizer and elevator are shown in this photograph. Note that both elevators had a trim tab.

ARMAMENT DETAILS

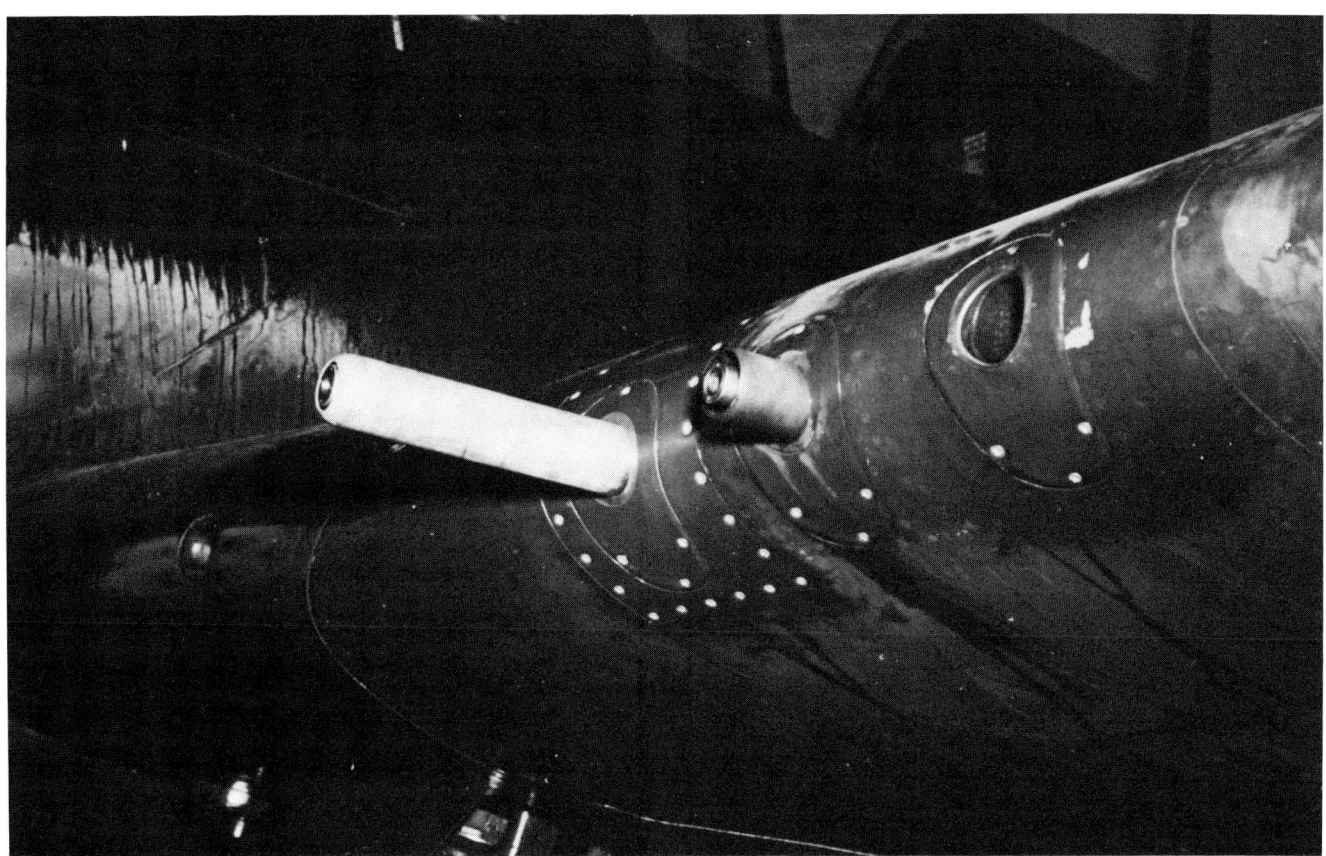

Above: Standard armament for most Hellcats was six .50 caliber Colt/Browning machine guns. Three were located in each wing in a staggered arrangement as shown here. (Grumman)

Right: Ejector slots for the shells were located under the wings. These are the slots under the right wing of an F6F-5.

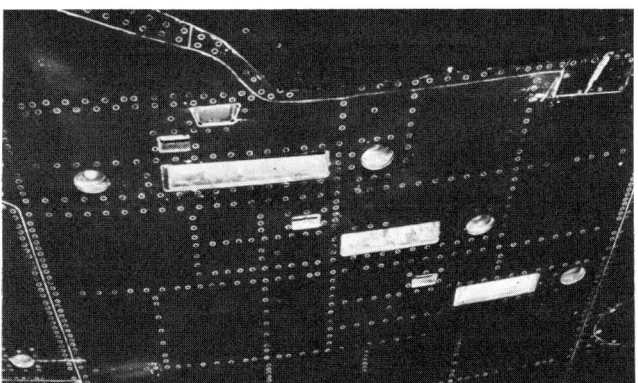

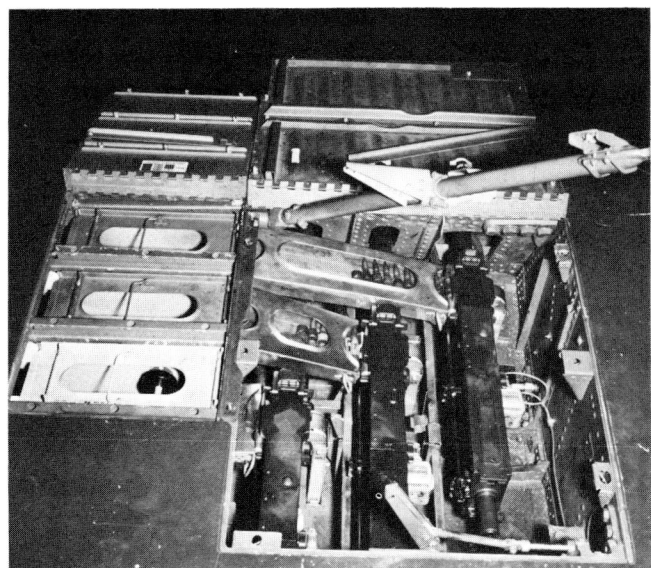

This photograph reveals the three guns in the left wing. Ammunition boxes are located in their proper positions, and a few cartridges are visible in the chutes for the two inner guns. (Grumman)

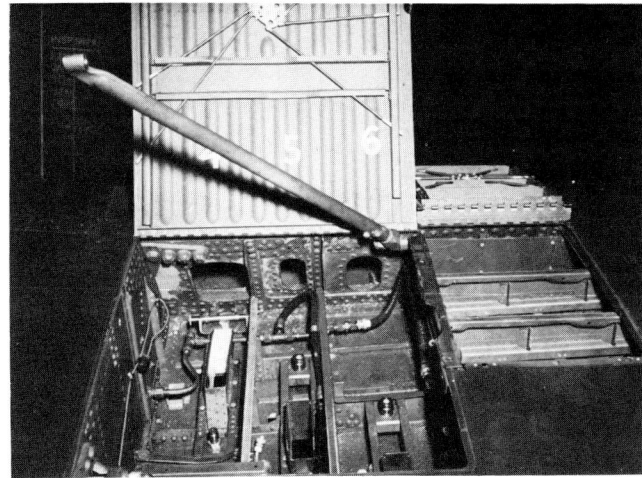

This is the gun bay in the right wing with the guns and ammunition boxes removed. (Grumman)

XF6F-1

The XF6F-1 is seen at Grumman's Bethpage, Long Island, plant shortly after completion. Note the exhaust details, the large landing gear covers, pitot tube on top of the right wing tip, and the spinner on the prop. The installed engine was a Wright 2600-16 with a Curtiss Electric prop. This combination provided 1600 horsepower at 2400 RPM.
(Grumman)

This front view of the XF6F-1 shows details of the engine, propeller, and wing fold. The lower cowl flaps are also visible. (Grumman)

These two photographs show details of the larger landing gear door that was originally installed on the prototypes. The design of the door was considerably changed on the production versions. (Both Grumman)

XF6F-2

One XF6F-2 was built and tested with two different powerplants with turbo-superchargers. These included the Wright R2600-15 and the Pratt and Whitney R2800-21. The performance was not as good as had been hoped for, and the turbo-supercharger was less than reliable. The aircraft, 66244, was later changed back to F6F-3 standards for delivery to the Navy. *(Grumman)*

The XF6F-2 is seen from below in this photograph. Many other details of the Hellcat's underside are visible here. *(Grumman)*

Above: This is the cockpit of the XF6F-2 as photographed on February 4, 1944. (Grumman)

Left: This close-up provides a good look at the name **Fuzzy Wuzzy** on the right side of the cowl. Also note the face above the name. The name came from the air flow indicators taped to the aircraft. (Grumman)

The large four-bladed prop of the XF6F-2 is illustrated in this photograph which was taken on February 7, 1944. (Grumman)

This in-flight view shows the exhaust of the turbo-supercharger under the fuselage. Note the name **Fuzzy Wuzzy** on the cowling. (Grumman)

These two photos reveal further details of the XF6F-2 on February 7, 1944. The name **Fuzzy Wuzzy** is only on the right side of the cowl. Note the large bare metal sections on both sides of the fuselage. (Both Grumman)

XF6F-3

The XF6F-3, 02982, was first flown on July 30, 1942. It was powered by the Pratt and Whitney R2800 engine, and was very similar to the XF6F-1, to include having the larger main landing gear covers. However, these did vary slightly in design from those on the XF6F-1. Differences included a smaller exhaust area just ahead of and above the wing, and a smaller pitot tube that was located under the right wing tip as it would be on production aircraft. (Grumman)

The six-position, blue disc and white star national insignia are visible in this view of the XF6F-3. (Grumman)

More details of the XF6F-3 are revealed in these two photographs. (Both Grumman)

Above and below: Front and rear views of the XF6F-3 provide a look at the remaining external details of the aircraft.
(Both Grumman)

The cockpit of the XF6F-3 is shown here. Compare this to the production cockpit in the F6F-3 illustrated beginning on page 24.
(Grumman)

F6F-3

The production F6F-3 is shown here with features common to the first examples produced. Note that the radio mast behind the cockpit is canted forward. Beginning with the 910th F6F-3, 65890, this was changed so that the mast was perpendicular to the centerline of the aircraft. It was located slightly to the right of centerline on the first 2560 F6F-3s, then slightly left of centerline beginning with BuNo 41295. As mentioned before, the gun fairings were only on the first production aircraft, extending through BuNo 26195. The landing light under the left wing (seen just inboard of the national insignia) was deleted after the 272nd F6F-3, which was BuNo 08885. The lower cowl flap was deleted on the 1265th example, which was BuNo 39999. The bulged fairing over the lateral exhaust is not present on this Hellcat.
(Grumman)

Taken on January 29, 1943, this photograph shows an early F6F-3 in flight. Again note the features of the early production aircraft as listed in the caption above. The aircraft is painted in the standard Navy scheme for that time period, consisting of non-specular blue/gray on the upper surfaces and sides, and light gray on the bottom. The aircraft in the photo at the top of this page is also in this paint scheme.
(Grumman)

Above: An excellent view of Hellcat details is provided in this photograph. The aircraft is tied down to the deck of an ESSEX class carrier. In the background is the most famous carrier of the war, the USS ENTERPRISE, CV-6.
(U.S. Navy via Grumman)

Left: Deck crewmen make checks on this F6F-3 as the aircraft is prepared for launch.
(U.S. Navy via Grumman)

Hellcats, Avengers, and Helldivers start their engines in preparation for a strike in mid-1944. The Grummans are characterized by their wings being folded back alongside their fuselages, while the Helldivers' wings fold overhead.
(U.S. Navy via Grumman)

This F6F-3 was painted overall yellow. The photograph is dated March 13, 1943. The aircraft was unarmed, and was used for radio controlled dive tests. It was later lost in an accident during one of these tests. *(Grumman)*

Radio gear and control cables are visible in the aft fuselage section of an F6F-3. The lead from the radio mast can be seen entering the fuselage at the top of the photograph, which is dated February 10, 1943. *(Grumman)*

This F6F-3 wears the three-tone paint scheme consisting of dark blue upper surfaces, intermediate blue fuselage sides and vertical tail, and white undersides. The national insignia has the short-lived red surround, and is a four-position arrangement instead of the earlier six-position variety. In the four-position arrangement, the insignia was deleted from the underside of the left wing and the top side of the right wing. (Grumman)

The centerline fuel tank is present on this early F6F-3. Note the gun fairings and lower cowl flap. (Grumman)

Hellcats form the backdrop to an inspection formation for the crew of this CVL. Another CVL can be seen in the background. Hellcats usually teamed with Avengers to form the air groups of the CVLs, and also flew from some CVEs. (U.S. Navy via Grumman)

With a five-inch gun firing in the background, Hellcats are seen being prepared for launch from the USS YORKTOWN, CV-10. The carrier in the distance appears to be the USS ENTERPRISE. (U.S. Navy via Grumman)

F6F-3 COCKPIT DETAILS

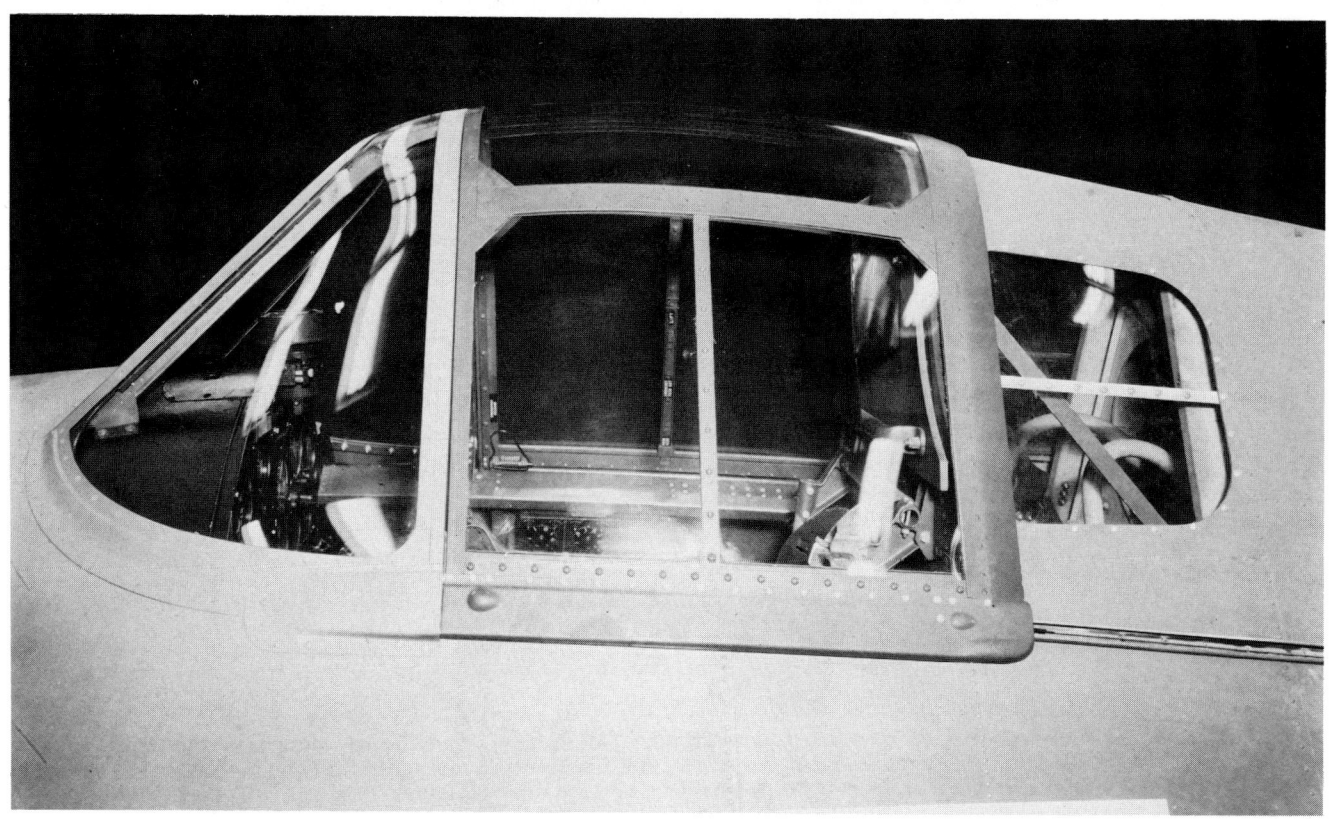

Details of the Hellcat's windshield, sliding canopy, and rear-vision window are seen here. The framework for the bullet-resistant glass in the front of the windshield is also visible. This is the style of windscreen used on the F6F-3N and the F6F-5. (Grumman)

The seat, shoulder harness, and lap belt are seen in this view looking straight down into the cockpit.
(Grumman)

This photograph is of the same aircraft as seen at left, and the camera location is the same. However, the seat has now been removed, and more details are visible.
(Grumman)

The instrument panel center console, and rudder pedals in F6F-3, 04875, are visible in this photo. There are only ten major instruments on the main instrument panel. Note the name **Grumman** on the rudder pedals. The Hellcat's cockpit was considered comfortable and well laid out. (Grumman)

The left side of the cockpit includes the throttle and mixture controls, trim controls, cowl and oil cooler flap switches, wing flap switch, and landing gear lever. Take-off and landing check lists are inscribed on a panel above the landing gear lever. (Grumman)

The right side of the cockpit had more of the traditional console arrangement. Keys for the entire cockpit of the F6F-3 are found on the following page. (Grumman)

F6F-3 COCKPIT KEYS

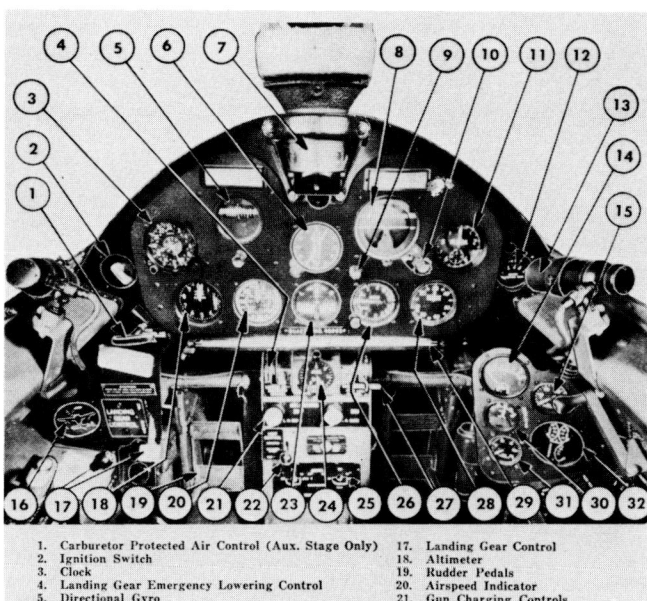

1. Carburetor Protected Air Control (Aux. Stage Only)
2. Ignition Switch
3. Clock
4. Landing Gear Emergency Lowering Control
5. Directional Gyro
6. Compass
7. Gunsight
8. Attitude Gyro
9. Chartboard Light
10. Attitude Gyro Caging Knob
11. Tachometer
12. Water Quantity Gage—A.D.I. System
13. Instrument Panel Fluorescent Light
14. Cylinder Head Temperature Gage
15. Oil Pressure Gage
16. Landing Gear & Wing Flap Position Indicator
17. Landing Gear Control
18. Altimeter
19. Rudder Pedals
20. Airspeed Indicator
21. Gun Charging Controls
22. Cockpit Heater Control
23. Turn and Bank Indicator
24. Ammunition Rounds Counter
25. Fluorescent Lights Control
26. Rate of Climb Indicator
27. Wing Lock Safety Control Handle
28. Manifold Pressure Gage
29. Chartboard
30. Oil-In Temperature Gage
31. Fuel Pressure Gage
32. Fuel Quantity Gages

INSTRUMENT PANEL

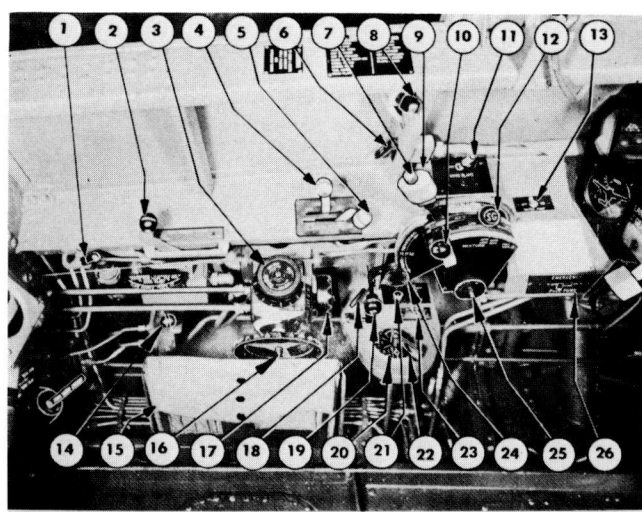

1. Lower Left Cockpit Light
2. Tail Wheel Lock Control
3. Rudder Trim Tab Control
4. Cowl Flaps Control
5. Oil Cooler-Intercooler Shutters Control
6. Droppable Fuel Tank Release Switch
7. Mask Microphone Switch
8. Upper Left Cockpit Light
9. Throttle Control
10. Mixture Control
11. Wing Flap Electrical Switch
12. Supercharger Control
13. Water Injection Control Switch
14. Wing Flap Manual Control
15. Map Case
16. Elevator Trim Tab Control
17. Aileron Trim Tab Control
18. Fuel Tank Pressurizing Control
19. Propeller Pitch Control
20. Fuel Selector Valve Dialface
21. Reserve Fuel Tank Pressurizing Control
22. Fuel Tank Selector Valve Control
23. Oil Dilution Switch
24. Propeller Pitch Vernier Control
25. Engine Control Quadrant Friction Knob
26. Auxiliary Electric Fuel Pump Switch

1. Cabin Sliding Hood Control
2. Battery Switch
3. Main Electrical Distribution Panel
4. Electrical Panel Light
5. Radio Controls
6. Recognition Lights
7. Hand Pump Selector Valve
8. Aft Right Cockpit Shelf Light
9. Hydraulic System Pressure Gage
10. Wing Locking Hydraulic Dump Pressure Gage
11. Wing Locking Hydraulic Control
12. Manual Reset Circuit Breaker Panel
13. Access to Reverse Current Relay
14. Hydraulic Hand Pump
15. Armament Panel
16. Hand Microphone
17. Pyrotechnic Cartridge Clips
18. Pyrotechnic Pistol Retainer
19. Radio Controls
20. IFF Destruction Switch
21. IFF Equipment Support

LEFT SIDE   RIGHT SIDE

MIXED GUN BATTERY

Above: A mixed battery of one 20mm cannon and two .50 caliber machine guns was tested on this late F6F-3. This armament combination was not adopted for the standard Hellcat fighters, but was used on many F6F-5N night fighters. (Grumman)

Right: This is a close-up view of the 20mm installation in the left wing. The cannon simply replaced the inboard .50 caliber gun in each wing. The two other guns remained as they had been in the standard six .50 caliber installation. (Grumman)

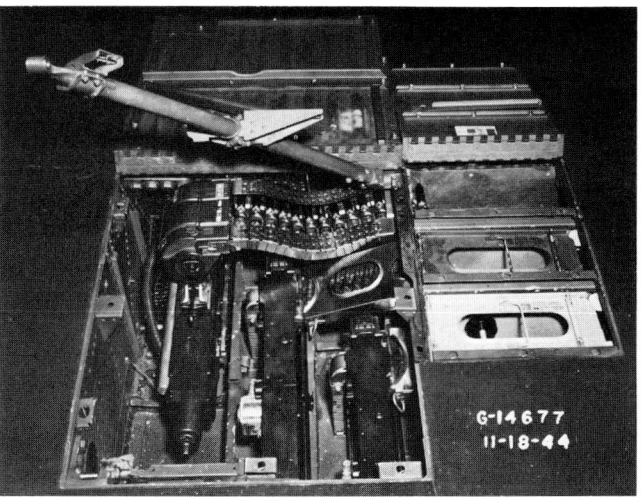

These two photographs show the mixed gun battery in each wing. Notice the larger feed belt for the 20mm cartridges as compared with the .50 caliber chutes. (Grumman)

F6F-3N

The F6F-3N night fighter version of the Hellcat was simply a standard F6F-3 with an AN/APS-6 radar mounted on the starboard wing. The antenna was faired into a radome, and other associated equipment was located inside the fuselage. Approximately two hundred examples were built, and the first entered service in November 1943. (Grumman)

Night-fighting Hellcats often worked in consort with an Avenger, as seen here. It was during one of these operations that Medal of Honor winner Butch O'Hare was lost in action. (U.S. Navy Grumman)

Details of the radar fairing are visible in this close-up photograph. (Grumman)

The armament for the -3N remained the standard six .50 caliber machine guns. (Grumman)

Above and below: These two photographs show the radar scope installed in the center of the instrument panel in an F6F-3N.
(Grumman)

F6F-3E

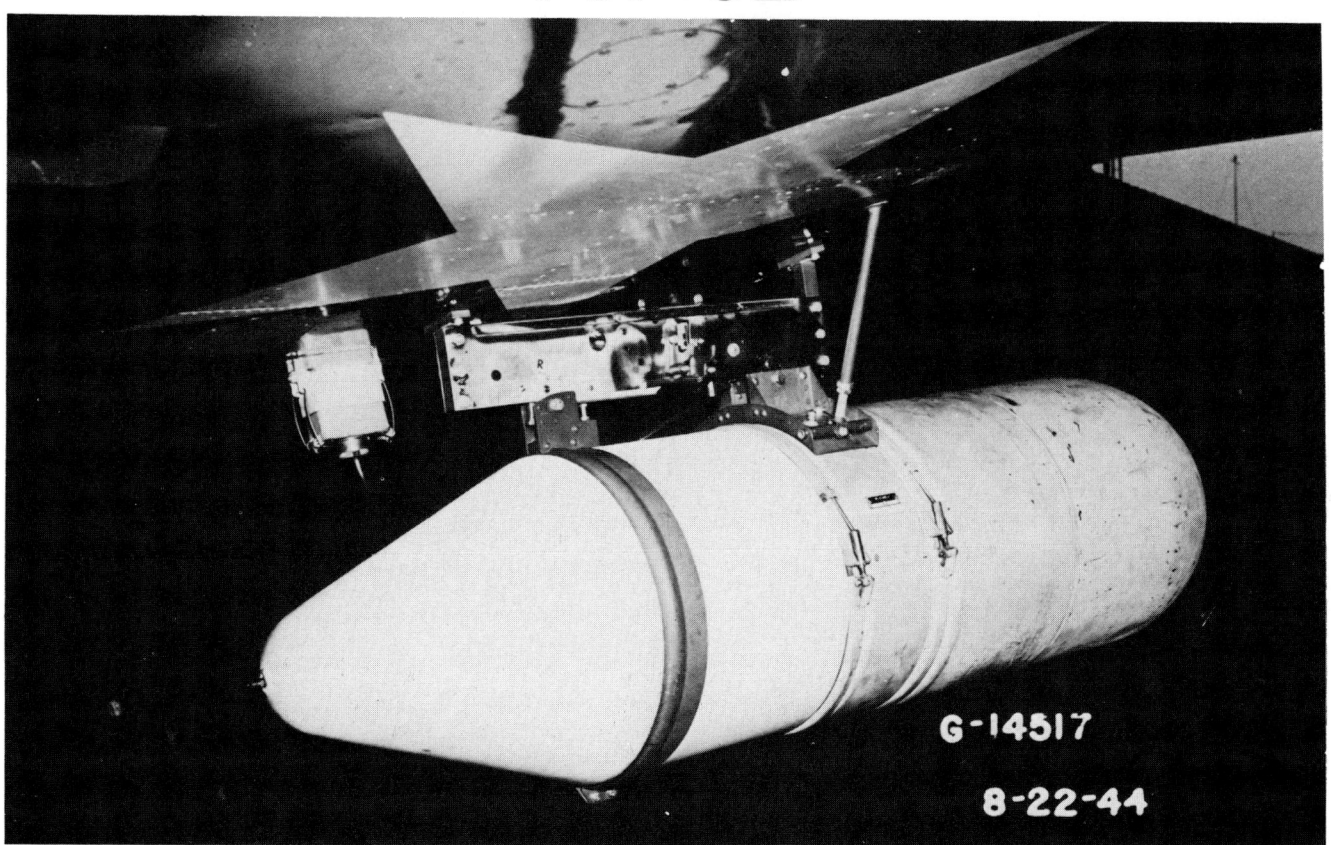

The other -3 night fighter version was the F6F-3E, but only eighteen of these were built. An AN/APS-4 radar was housed in a pod beneath the right wing rather than being in a fairing. *(Grumman)*

Radio equipment for the AN/APS-4 was located in the fuselage. *(Grumman)*

The radar scope in the F6F-3E was considerably different than that used with the AN/APS-6 in the -3N.
(Grumman)

Radar operating controls were located on the left side of the cockpit. (Grumman)

The right side of the cockpit remained virtually the same as it was in the standard F6F-3. (Grumman)

XF6F-4

The first Hellcat XF6F-1 prototype, 02981, was used as a test bed for the XF6F-4. This version replaced the six .50 caliber machine guns with four 20mm cannon, and was powered by a Pratt and Whitney R2800-27 engine. The aircraft was flown for the first time in this configuration on October 3, 1942, but was never accepted for production. It was subsequently converted to a standard F6F-3 and delivered to the Navy. (Grumman)

This is the instrument panel in the XF6F-4. (Grumman)

HELLCAT COLORS

Left: Three color schemes were used on Hellcats during the World War II years. The first one was used only a short time on the F6F, and consisted of non-specular blue/gray (FS 36118) on the upper surfaces, and non-specular light gray (FS 36440) on the undersides. The national insignia was a dark blue disc with a white star, and it was located in six positions on the aircraft. This was the standard scheme used on Navy fighters at the time the Hellcat entered service, but it was soon replaced by the three-tone scheme seen below. (Grumman)

Above center: The three-tone scheme consisted of non-specular blue (FS 35042) on the upper surfaces, non-specular intermediate blue (FS 35164) on the sides and vertical tail, and flat white on the undersides. A white bar was added to each side of the national insignia, and for a short time in 1943 the entire insignia had a red surround. Later this was replaced with dark blue around the bars, and the red was deleted. This insignia was located in only four places on the aircraft, being deleted from the underside of the left wing and the top of the right wing. However, exceptions to this rule did exist. (Grumman)

Right: The final paint scheme on the Hellcat was overall glossy sea blue (FS 15042). There was no separate blue disk around the stars or blue outline around the bars in the insignia since the plane itself was dark blue. For a time, white geometric shapes designated the carrier to which an aircraft was assigned, and these were later replaced with letters. Note the antenna offset to the left of centerline just behind the canopy.
(National Archives via Piet)

ON THE CARRIERS

Above left and right: Photographs like these, showing aircraft positioned next to the superstructures of their carriers, were very popular during the war, and have often been published. At left is an early F6F-3 on the USS YORKTOWN, CV-10, in May 1943. The aircraft is in the blue/gray over light gray scheme. The deck crewmen are ready to pull the chocks from the wheels as the aircraft is prepared for launching. At right is another F6F-3 in a worn three-tone scheme. The photograph was taken aboard the USS YORKTOWN in August 1943. Although almost indistinguishable in the photograph, there is a small **00** under the horizontal tail, indicating that this is the CAG's aircraft. (Left National Archives via Piet, right U.S. Navy via Grumman)

Left: This Hellcat is taxiing forward after landing aboard the USS LEXINGTON, CV-16. Note the raised barriers behind the aircraft. (National Archives via Piet)

These two flight deck scenes were taken aboard the USS YORKTOWN, CV-10. At left, several F6F-3s warm up prior to launch, and at right, Hellcats are being respotted by deck crewmen on the aft end of the flight deck.
(Both National Archives via Piet)

Hellcats, with wings folded, are positioned in front of SBD Dauntless dive bombers on the flight deck of the USS ESSEX, CV-9. Aircraft are in the blue/gray over light gray scheme, indicating that this photo was probably taken during the first half of 1943. (U.S. Navy via Grumman)

*An F6F-3 is being hoisted aboard a carrier in this photo. **V5** is on the wing, and part of the red surround is visible around the national insignia on the fuselage. Note the tape on the guns, and the bomb rack on the center section of the wing. It is visible just under the guns.* (U.S. Navy via Grumman)

The flight deck officer gives the signal to pull the chocks as this F6F-3 is readied for launch. (U.S. Navy via Grumman)

These two photographs show Hellcats and Avengers aboard the USS COWPENS, CVL-25, during the raids on the Gilbert Islands. Note the variations in the color schemes and markings on the aircraft. Air groups on the CVLs were usually comprised of Hellcats and Avengers, meaning that every plane on the ship was a Grumman product, although many Avengers were actually built by General Motors as TBMs. (Both National Archives via Piet)

HELLCAT DRONES

After the war, many Hellcats served as drones. These aircraft were usually painted in very colorful schemes and markings. This is an F6F-5K, which was photographed at NAS Atlantic City on March 13, 1946. This aircraft and several others were used in the atomic bomb tests known as "Operation Crossroads." (National Archives via Piet)

These two photographs show more of the Hellcat drones used in "Operation Crossroads." Note that each aircraft had a different colored tail and a different tail number. (Both National Archives via Piet)

This F6F-3K is pictured at NAS Johnsville, Pennsylvania, in 1945. The close-up at right provides a look at the insignia on the cowling. (Both Arnold/NASM via Piet)

F6F-5K

Hellcat drones were also used as flying bombs against communist targets during the Korean War. Here an F6F-5K is being readied for launch from the USS BOXER, CV-21, while the control plane, a Douglas Skyraider, is launched from the starboard catapult.
(National Archives via Piet)

This drone was used for static firings of the Sparrow I air-to-air missile at Point Mugu. A black pylon was located under the right wing. In the photo at right, the missile is in place. Bon Ami cleaner was rubbed on the underside of the wing to register the blast pattern of the missile. Also see page 53 for more details of these tests.
(Both National Archives via Piet)

HELLCAT DETAILS IN COLOR
F6F-3 COCKPIT COLORS

The instrument panel in an F6F-3 can be seen here. The cockpit was chromate green with flat black panels. Only ten instruments were on this main panel. See the rear cover for another photograph of this instrument panel.

The left side of the cockpit is shown here. Check off lists for take off and landing are printed on a small placard on the cockpit rail.

Details of the right side of the cockpit are shown here. Radio gear, electric and hydraulic controls, and IFF equipment are located on this side of the cockpit. The small auxiliary panel at the front end of the right console has not been installed in this restored aircraft, but it would be the same as the one shown for the F6F-5 in the bottom photo on the next page.

There was no center console on the main instrument panel. Instead, there was a separate pedestal which was lower and several inches further forward than the panel. The red handle at the top left is the emergency landing gear lowering lever, while the red handle at right is the wing lock safety control handle. Below these are the gun chargers. Heater and fresh air controls are at the bottom of this pedestal. Details of the right rudder pedal can also be seen in this photo.

The metal seat, lap belts, and shoulder harnesses can be seen in this view.

F6F-5 COCKPIT COLORS

Above: The instrument panel in the F6F-5 was very similar to that in the earlier -3. Although the clock is missing from this panel, it would be essentially the same as the one shown for the F6F-3 on the previous page.

Left: The left side of the F6F-5 cockpit is illustrated here.

This is the right side of the cockpit. Note the auxiliary panel at the forward end of the console. This panel would also be the same in an F6F-3, although it is missing from the restored aircraft shown on the previous page. Details of one of the rudder pedals is visible here.

PRATT & WHITNEY R2800 ENGINE COLORS

 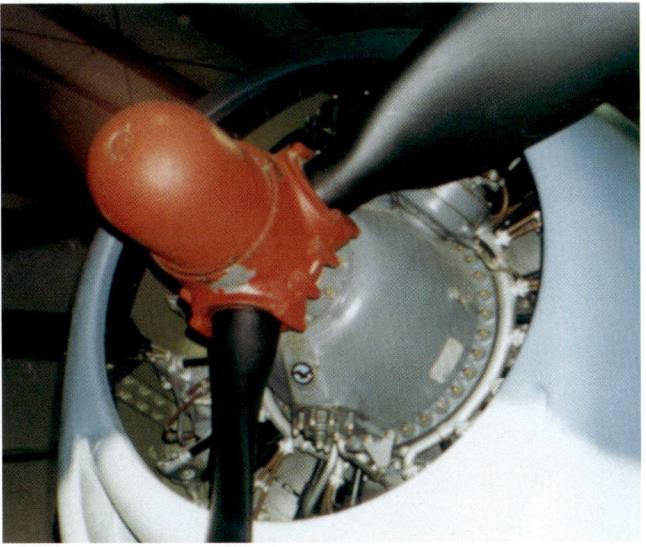

These two photos show the Pratt & Whitney R2800 engine installed in two different Hellcats. At left is an F6F-5 and at right is an F6F-3. Details and colors are essentially the same. Note the chromate green on the inside of the cowling. The colorful Pratt & Whitney emblem is also visible on each engine.

With all cowling parts removed, almost all of the engine's details become visible in these two photographs. This Hellcat was photographed while under restoration at the Planes of Fame Museum at Chino, California.

Left and right side views of the engine accessory compartment provide a look at even more engine details. The interior of this compartment is basically chromate green. Also visible is the area just behind the aft row of cylinders. Some of the exhaust piping has not yet been installed.

DIMENSIONS

DIMENSION	ACTUAL	1/72nd SCALE	1/48th SCALE	1/32nd SCALE
Wingspan	42' 10"	7.14"	10.71"	16.06"
Length	33' 7 "	5.60"	8.40"	12.60"
Height (3 Point)	11' 7 "	1.93"	2.90"	4.34"
Stabilizer Span	18' 6 "	3.08"	4.63"	6.94"
Wheel Track	11' 0 "	1.83"	2.75"	4.13"
Prop Diameter	13' 1 "	2.18"	3.27"	4.91"

DETAIL & SCALE 1/72ND FIVE-VIEW DRAWINGS

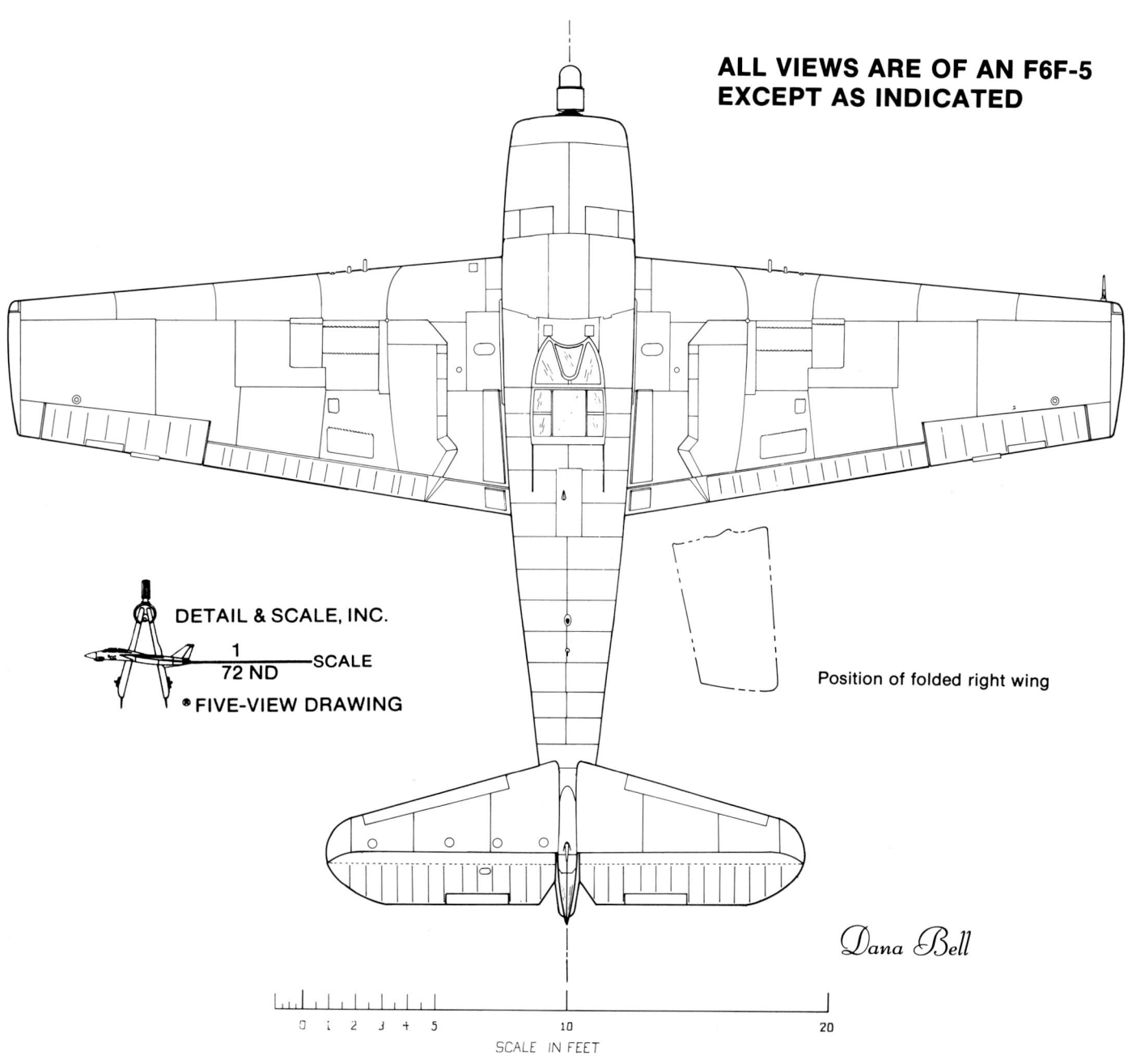

ALL VIEWS ARE OF AN F6F-5 EXCEPT AS INDICATED

Position of folded right wing

DETAIL & SCALE, INC.
1/72 ND SCALE
FIVE-VIEW DRAWING

Dana Bell

SCALE IN FEET

Front view rotates around fuselage reference line, not thrust line.

Position of folded wings

DETAIL & SCALE, INC.
$\frac{1}{72\text{ ND}}$ SCALE
• FIVE-VIEW DRAWING

Dana Bell

Metal cover on underside of flaps for all aircraft with RP (rocket) installation. MK V-1 installation is shown.

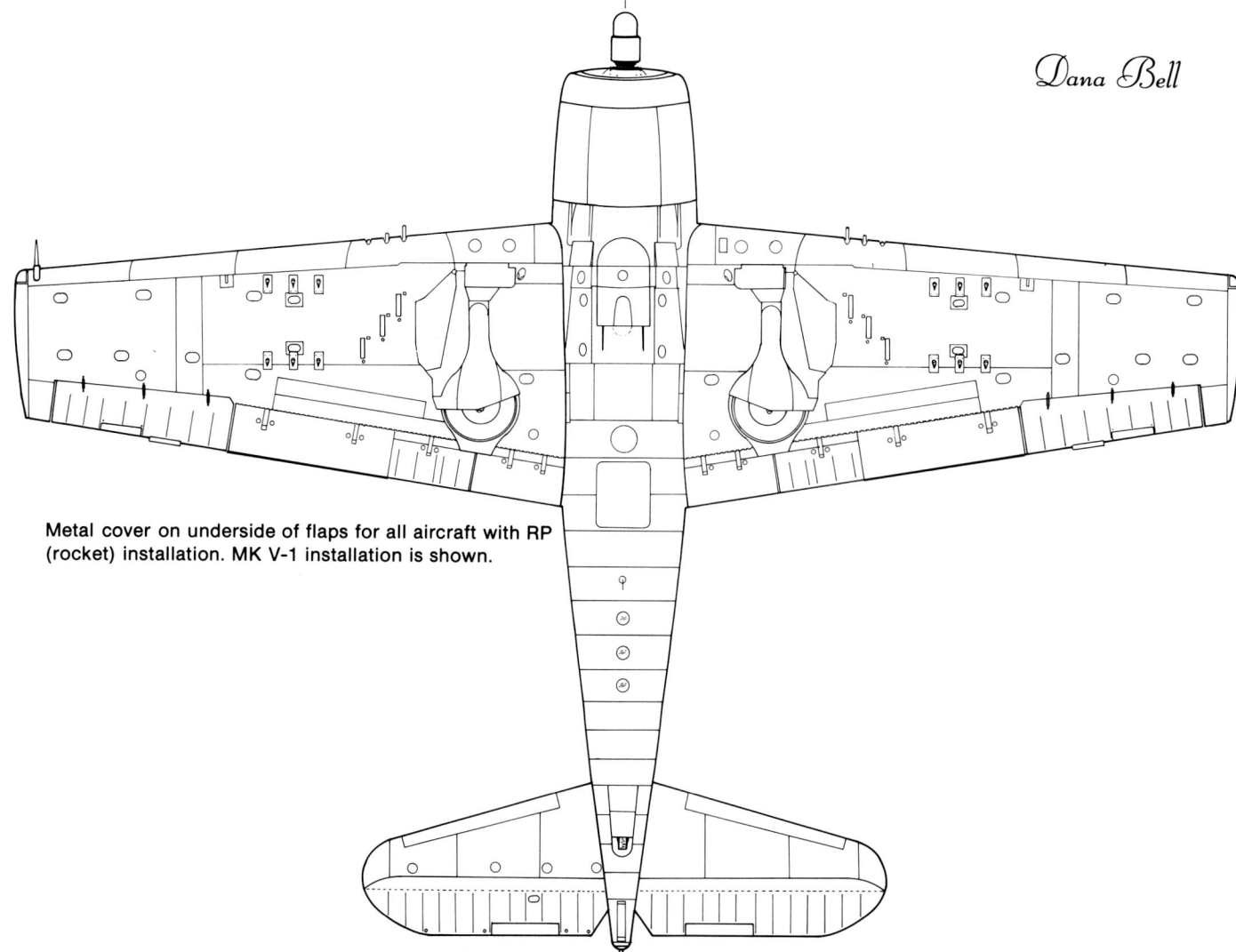

Dana Bell

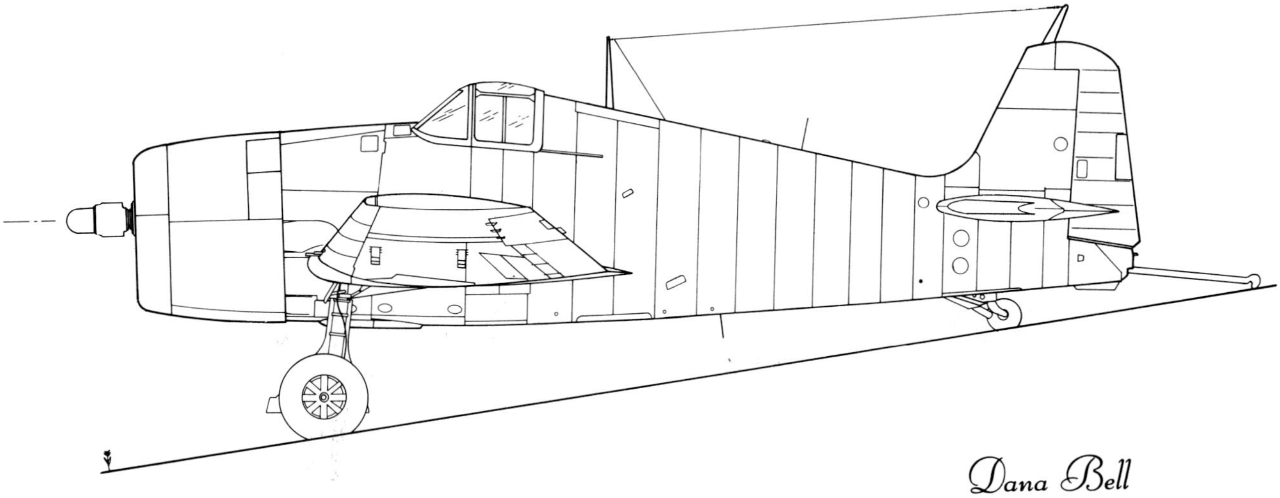

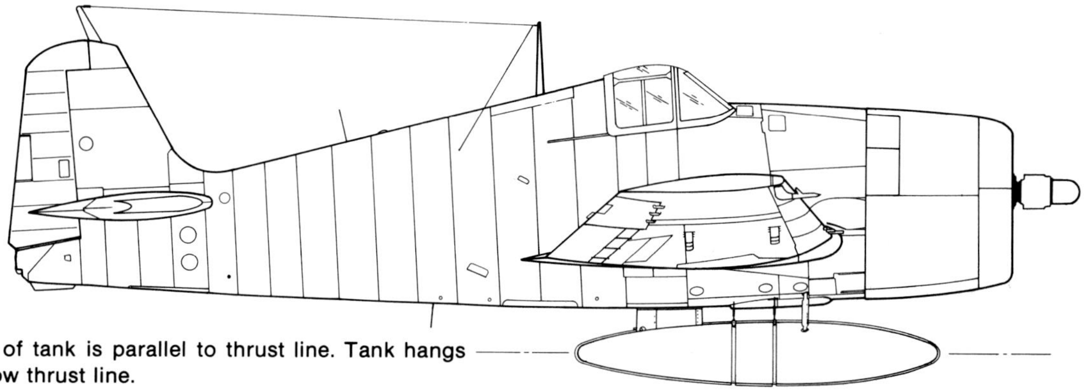

Centerline of tank is parallel to thrust line. Tank hangs 61.25" below thrust line.

Tanks 28301 (aluminum) and 28350 (steel) are interchangeable. Useable tank capacity is 150 gallons.

Use tank on:

F6F-3	26087 & up
F6F-3N	26104 & up
F6F-5	58107 & up
F6F-5N	58100 & up

DETAIL & SCALE, INC.

1/72 ND SCALE

® FIVE-VIEW DRAWING

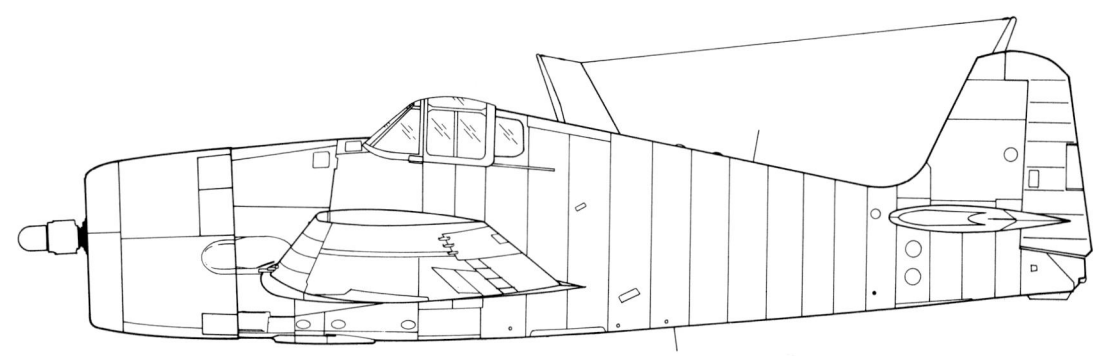

F6F-3 LEFT SIDE VIEW

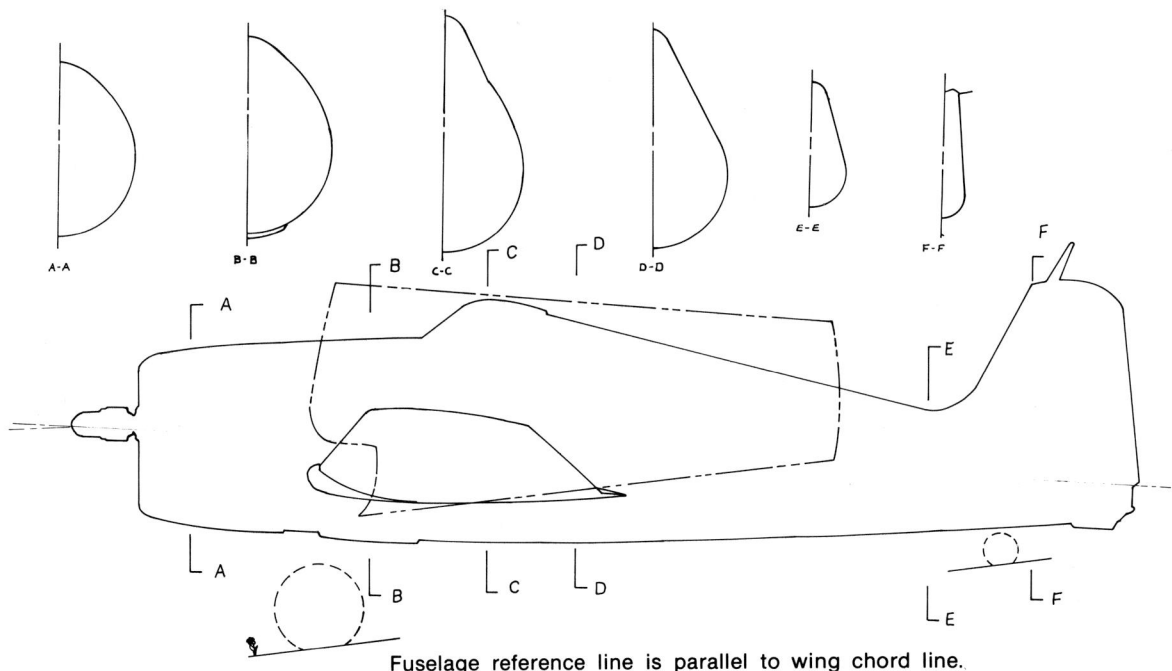

Fuselage reference line is parallel to wing chord line. Thrust line and cowl reference lines deflect three degrees down.

Dana Bell

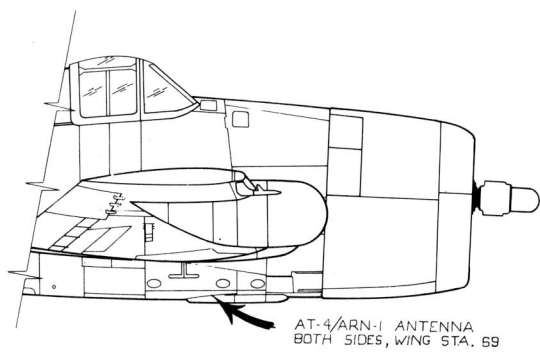

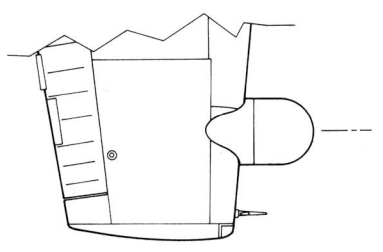

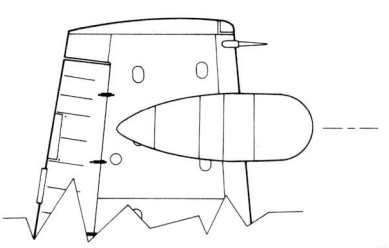

F6F-3/5N AN/APS-6 RADAR FAIRING

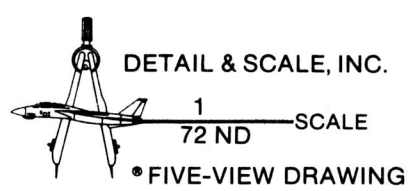

DETAIL & SCALE, INC.

1/72ND SCALE

® FIVE-VIEW DRAWING

RADAR INSTALLATIONS

AIA	F6F-3N	08945 - 66232
AIA	F6F-3N	40010 - 41510
		(except 41302)
AIA	F6F-3N	41764 - 43120
AIA	F6F-5N	58004 - 58641
AN/APS-6A	F6F-5N	58642
AIA	F6F-5N	58643 - 58959
AN/APS-6A	F6F-5N	58960
AIA	F6F-5N	58961 - 58989
AN/APS-6A	F6F-5N	70038 - 72991
AN/APS-6A	F6F-5N	77349 - 77671
AN/APS-6	F6F-5N	77680 - 77748
AN/APS-6A	F6F-5N	77749
AN/APS-6	F6F-5N	77750 - 77756
AN/APS-6A	F6F-5N	77757
AN/APS-6	F6F-5N	77758 - 77791
AN/APS-6A	F6F-5N	77827 - 77960
AN/APS-6	F6F-5N	77968 thru end

AIA: Sperry
AN/APS-6: Dalmo-Victor Westinghouse
AN/APS-6A: Dalmo-Victor Philco

Nacelle mounted on right wing only, 214 7/16" from aircraft centerline.

F6F-5

One of the first F6F-5s sits on the ramp at Bethpage. It has the small windows behind the cockpit which had been used on the -3, but this feature was deleted on later -5s. The introduction of the -5 came about at the same time as the Navy was changing to the overall glossy sea blue scheme. (Grumman)

Five F6F-5s are seen in post-war markings. The red bar has been added to the national insignia. (National Archives)

A factory-fresh F6F-5 is shown parked outside Grumman's plant. This is a later production aircraft than the one in the photograph at the top of the page, as indicated by the lack of the windows behind the cockpit. (Grumman)

F6F-5s from Advanced Training Unit 102 are seen here in flight after the war. (Grumman)

Hellcats, Hellcats, and more Hellcats! In March 1945, Grumman produced over 600 Hellcats. The production rate actually got so high that the Navy asked Grumman to cut back. This was a benefit of an outstanding effort by Grumman and its employees, and the fact that America never had its production facilities bombed during the war. Grumman produced all of the Hellcats built, unlike the Wildcat and Avenger that were also built by General Motors. These two photographs show Hellcats parked outside the Grumman plant. In all, 12,273 Hellcats of all types were produced. (Both Grumman)

10,000th HELLCAT

The 10,000th Hellcat, previously seen on page 6, was specially marked and delivered to its carrier in a special ceremony. **10,000th HELLCAT** was painted in white on both sides of the cowling. Here it is seen landing aboard the USS TICONDEROGA, CV-14, where it was assigned to VBF-87. (Grumman)

This photograph, taken before the aircraft left Bethpage, shows special markings on one of the propeller blades. Note that the **76**, seen on the cowl and forward landing gear doors in the other photographs, had not been added yet. Also note that the color of the propeller hub is different. (Grumman)

With unit markings now added, the Navy takes delivery of the Hellcat aboard the USS TICONDEROGA. (Grumman)

F6F-5 COCKPIT DETAILS

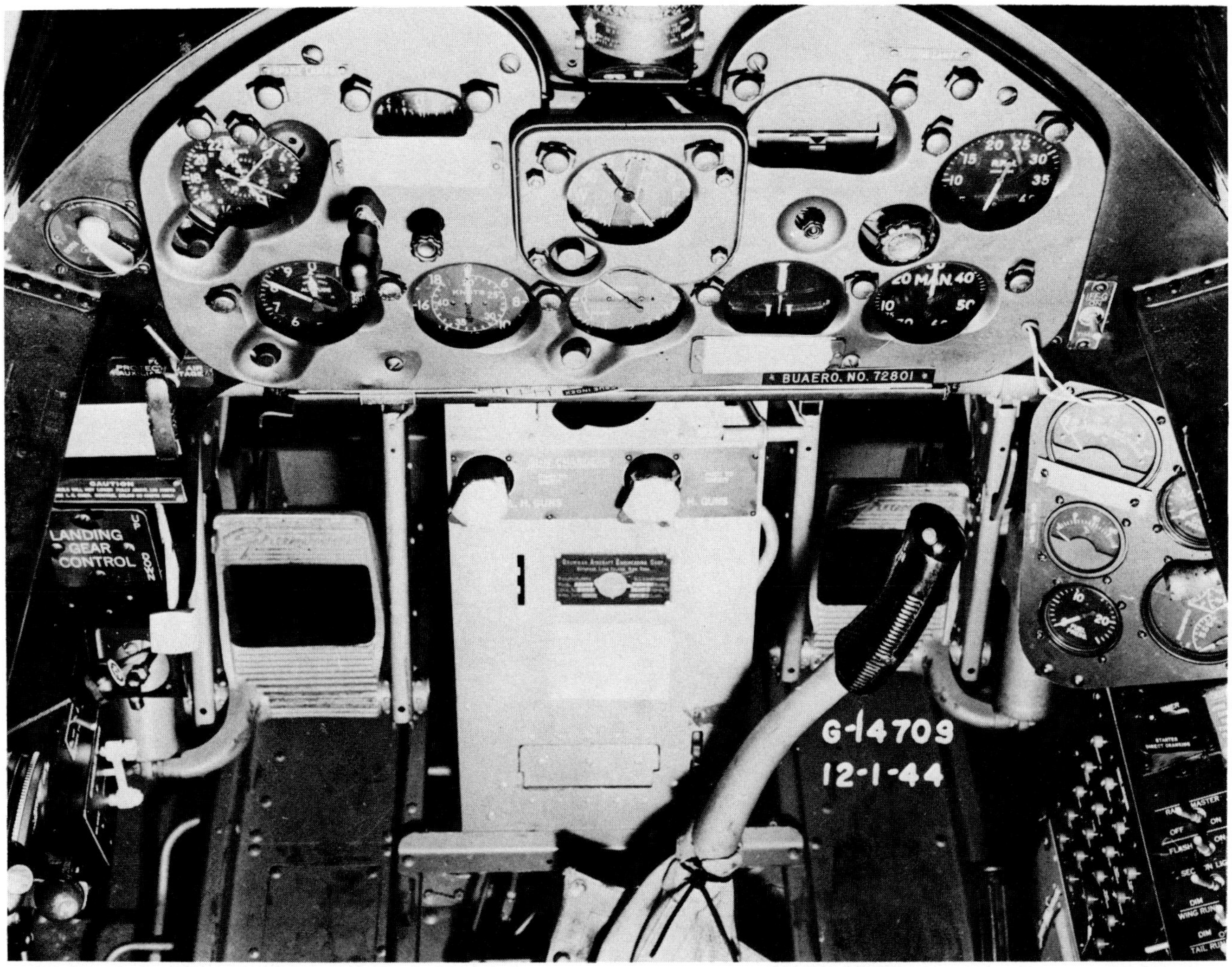

BUAERO. NO. 72801
CAUTION
LANDING GEAR CONTROL
UP
DOWN
H. GUNS
H. GUNS
G-14709
12-1-44
MASTER
ON
OFF
FLASH
DIM
WING RUN
DIM
TAIL RUN

Details of the front instrument panel and center console are visible in this photograph. *(Grumman)*

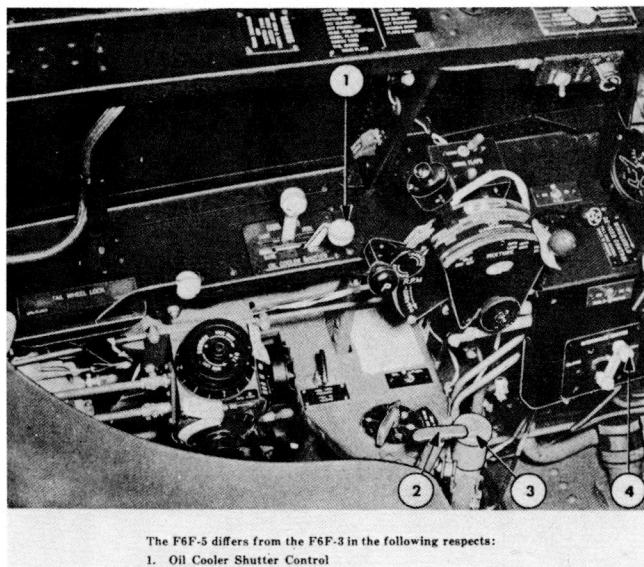

1
2
3
4
The F6F-5 differs from the F6F-3 in the following respects:
1. Oil Cooler Shutter Control
2. Fuselage Droppable Tank Manual Release Control
3. Anti-Blackout Regulator
4. Intercooler Shutter Control
5. Removal of the Fuel Level Warning Light

This is the left side of the cockpit in an F6F-5. The circled numbers point out the differences from the F6F-3. *(Grumman)*

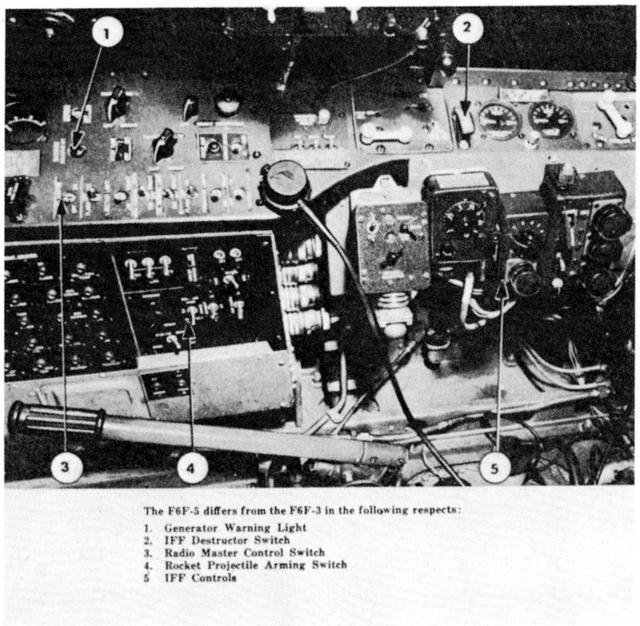

1
2
3
4
5
The F6F-5 differs from the F6F-3 in the following respects:
1. Generator Warning Light
2. IFF Destructor Switch
3. Radio Master Control Switch
4. Rocket Projectile Arming Switch
5 IFF Controls

The right side of the F6F-5 cockpit is shown here. Again, most features remain as they were in the -3, but five differences are noted. *(Grumman)*

Each aircraft was thoroughly checked out and test flown before delivery to the Navy. Here a F6F-5, with its production number on the cowling, is being run up during engine tests. (Grumman)

Although fairly quickly replaced with more advanced fighters after the war, and then by the first jets, the Hellcat did continue to serve on for some time. Here F6F-5s fly over the USS LEYTE, CV-32. In the background is the USS MIDWAY, CVB-41, and an unidentified ESSEX class carrier. (U.S. Navy via Grumman)

The F6F-5 had a different windshield than the F6F-3. Part of the overhead framework was deleted, and the forward part of the windshield was bullet-resistant glass. On the F6F-3, the bullet-resistant glass was a separate piece inside the windshield. This design was also used on the F6F-3N night fighter. (Grumman)

Although over 12,000 Hellcats were built, only a handful still exist. F6F-5, 79863, was one of the lucky ones. These two photos show it being removed from storage for restoration to flying condition. (Both Grumman)

F6F-5N/E NIGHT FIGHTERS

As was the case with the F6F-3, night fighter -5N and -5E versions were made using the F6F-5 as a basis. As before, the AN/APS-4 radar was used on the F6F-5E and the AN/APS-6 was fitted in the -5N, which was the more prevalent version. This is an F6F-5N with the radar fairing installed in its starboard wing. (Grumman)

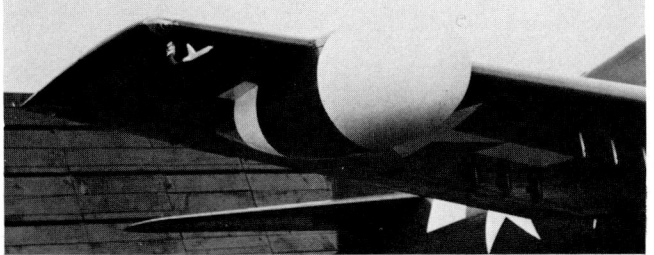 

These close-ups show the AN/APS-6 radar fairing in better detail. Note the white bar of the national insignia extending on the radome. (Both Grumman)

The mixed gun battery shown on page 27 was usually used on the F6F-5N. Flash hiders were often placed on the guns and exhausts to keep from blinding the pilot. However, they are not present in this photo. (Grumman)

XF6F-6

Had the war lasted longer than it did, the F6F-6 would probably have been the third production Hellcat. Two prototypes were built by modifying airframes 70188 and 70913. The first XF6F-6 made its maiden flight on July 6, 1944, and achieved a top speed of 417 mph. A Pratt and Whitney R2800-18W engine was installed, and was fitted with a Hamilton Standard four-bladed propeller. This is a front view of the first XF6F-6. (Grumman)

The basic lines that had been designed into the Hellcat since day one remained the same for the XF6F-6. (Grumman)

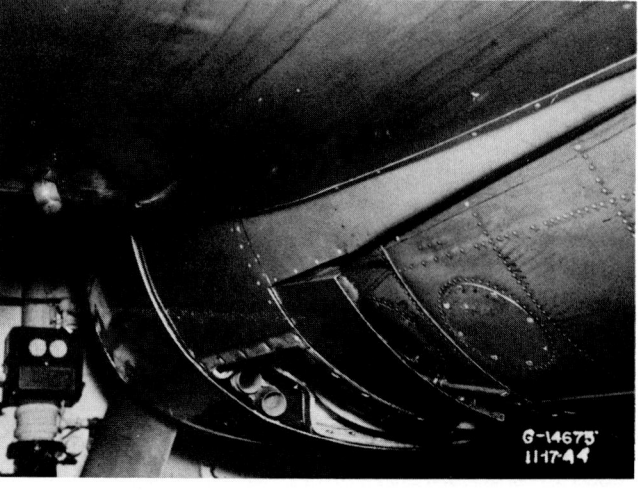

The tight-fitting cowl and the exhaust of the XF6F-6 are visible in these two views. (Grumman)

The instrument panel, center console, and rudder pedals of the XF6F-6 are shown in this photo. Note the torquemeter located at the center top of the instrument panel. It was used only for test purposes. (Grumman)

These left and right side views of the XF6F-6 cockpit show that little was changed from the earlier models of the Hellcat. (Both Grumman)

HELLCAT DRONES

Hellcat drones were first designated with the suffix **D**, and then later with **K**. Extra antennas appeared on the spine of the aircraft, and were associated with the radio control gear that was fitted. Wing tip tanks were installed on some of the drones. . This F6F-5K receives its last salute as the engine is run up by the pilot. (Grumman)

These two photographs show the markings of a red F6F-5K, which has had its wing tips modified for tanks. All markings are in white except the national insignia, which is the standard red, white, and blue. The anti-glare panel is flat black. (Grumman)

This F6F-5K put in an appearance at the Detroit Air Races in 1961. The wing tips are not modified on this aircraft. The markings are all in white, and the front of the cowling is yellow. The usual antennas associated with drones are missing from the spine. (Grumman)

SPARROW MISSILE TESTS

As shown in color on page 37, this former F6F-5 was used for test firings of the Sparrow I air-to-air missile. A camera pod to photograph the launch of the missile is mounted on the centerline station. (National Archives)

Missile and pylon details are visible here. Imagination could suggest what such armament would have done for the Hellcat's 19 to 1 kill ratio if it had been available in World War II! Of course, the Sparrow was not designed for the Hellcat, and would have affected flight performance. As a radar guided missile, it would have also required the Hellcat to carry a radar. Perhaps it is best that it was only used for test firings after all! (National Archives)

EXTERNAL STORES

In addition to its gun ordnance, the Hellcat was fitted with several types of external stores. HVAR 5-inch rockets were first tried under the wings of the F6F-3, and three zero-length rails for these rockets were standard under the wings of the F6F-5. This -5 carries six 5-inch HVARs and two Tiny Tim rockets under the wing center section.
(National Archives)

ROCKETS

A Tiny Tim is being test fired from this F6F-5.
(National Archives)

At left is a 2.75-inch rocket mounted on one of three rails under the left wing of an F6F-3. Such rails never became standard on U.S. Navy Hellcats, but were used on British F6Fs. At right is the same type of rocket on zero-length rails. The zero-length rails used for the 5-inch rockets were larger than these.
(Both Grumman)

BOMBS

As Hellcats made up larger and larger portions of carrier air groups, they displaced the dive and torpedo bombers. Therefore they were used to carry bombs up to the 1000-pound size. A 1000-pound bomb is shown on its dolly beneath the centerline of a Hellcat. *(Grumman)*

These two photographs show bombs attached to the centerline station. However, this station was usually used for the 150-gallon drop tank, while the bombs were carried on pylons beneath the center section of the wing. *(Both Grumman)*

The earlier style bomb rack is shown here on an F6F-3. The bomb appears to be a 500-pound general purpose type. *(Both Grumman)*

The later style bomb rack is shown here. The bombs are said to be fire bombs, but they are of different types. *(Both Grumman)*

TORPEDOES

It was logical to try to fit a torpedo under the Hellcat, and it was demonstrated that it could be carried successfully. However, bombs proved more successful than torpedos at sinking ships, and the aerial torpedoes in the U.S. Navy's inventory during World War II were not the most reliable weapons, to say the least. Therefore, the Hellcat never carried a torpedo in combat. (Grumman)

A torpedo and its loading dolly are shown here beneath an F6F-3. (Grumman)

At left is a head-on view of a loaded torpedo, and at right is a close-up of the attach point and suspending cables. (Both Grumman)

BRITISH HELLCATS

The Fleet Air Arm of the Royal Navy operated both the F6F-3 and F6F-5 versions of the Hellcat. Although originally named the Gannet, the British changed the name to Hellcat in January 1944. This is one of 252 F6F-3s supplied to the British under the Lend-Lease program. (Grumman)

There were 930 F6F-5s delivered to the British. This newly completed Hellcat awaits delivery to the Royal Navy outside Grumman's plant. (Grumman)

LCDR Edward Walthal of the Royal Navy checks out a British Hellcat at the U.S. East Coast Modification Center. (Grumman)

British women also got into the act. Here a Royal Navy WREN inspects an F6F-3. (Grumman)

INTERVIEW WITH DAVID McCAMPBELL

Note: Captain David McCampbell, USN (Retired), is the Navy's all-time leading ace with thirty-four confirmed air-to-air victories. All of these were attained while flying the Hellcat as the Commanding Officer of Carrier Air Wing 15 on the USS ESSEX (CV-9). After attending Georgia Tech for one year where he took up engineering and diving, Captain McCampbell transferred to the U.S. Naval Academy as a member of the class of 1933. While there, he was an intercollegiate diving champion, and was good enough to have been selected for the 1932 Olympics. However, priority went to academics, and he did not compete in the Olympic tryouts. Nine of his air-to-air victories came in a single mission on October 24, 1944, and for this he was awarded the Medal of Honor. His nine kills in a single mission is a record for all American and allied fighter pilots, and all of his thirty-four kills were scored during a single tour in combat. This is also a record. After the war, he remained in the Navy until 1964, and among his assignments was a tour as commanding officer of the USS BON HOMME RICHARD (CVA-31). The following interview was conducted at his home on September 9, 1987, just a few days before this book went to press. In it he discusses the Hellcat, his own experiences, and the markings on his personal aircraft. Questions asked by the author are in regular type, while Captain McCampbell's comments and answers are in bold type.

This is David McCampbell as a Commander and CAG-15. (McCampbell)

Let's start with the Hellcat itself. As someone who scored all of his kills in the Hellcat, what do you remember the most about the Hellcat as a fighter aircraft?
The Hellcat was an outstanding fighter plane. It performed well, was easy to fly, and was a stable gun platform. But what I really remember most was that it was rugged and easy to maintain. I usually landed first ahead of my wingman Roy Rushing. Once I had pulled forward and had gotten out of my aircraft as Roy landed and taxied forward. We gave a thumbs-up sign to the deck crew if the fighter was all right, and needed nothing other than refueling and rearming before being ready to go again. Here came Roy giving a thumbs-up, yet I could see his number nine piston pumping oil through the cylinder. The damage had not been even noticeable to him. That is what I mean by rugged. It could take a lot of punishment and still fly. Every one of my kills exploded or at least caught fire. The Hellcat just did not do that. And it was easy to maintain. I remember that our mechanics could change an entire engine in just four hours. Most parts of the aircraft were easily reachable, and simple to work on.

You had a chance to fly the F4U Corsair. How did it compare to the Hellcat?
The Corsair was a little faster, and had a little better rate of climb. I had a friend take up a Corsair and I flew a Hellcat. We flew some mock combat, and his speed and climb gave him a slight advantage. Both aircraft were great fighters.

I have read about other pilots in other fighters having problems with guns jamming. Did this ever happen to you in the Hellcat?
Never. My guns always performed perfectly. None of my pilots ever had problems with the guns unless he got real excited and damaged the barrels by firing too long of a burst. We boresighted our guns differently than what was officially approved by the Armament Bureau. We were set up so that niney-two or ninety-three percent of our rounds were in a three foot circle at 1000 feet. No aircraft could hope to withstand that.

I would expect that all of those bullets so tightly packed into a three foot circle would also do a lot of damage to a ship.
We actually did not get that close to a ship when attacking it. If there was anti-aircraft fire we would not go below 1500 feet, but although the bullets dispersed beyond 1000 feet, they still could do considerable damage.

How long of a burst did you usually fire?
No more than three to four seconds.

It has been said many times that the pilots with the best gunnery skills were often the ones that had hunted when

they were boys. Was this true in your case?
Oh yes. I had a shotgun when I was eleven, and did a lot of quail hunting. I used to hunt and shoot with Barry Goldwater (later the Senator from Arizona) **when he and I were in Staunton Military Academy together. Each of the Naval Air Stations had a skeet range, and I would do a lot of shooting when I had the chance.**

As CAG of Air Group 15, you also had TBF Avengers and SB2Cs in your squadrons. What did you think of those aircraft?
The SB2C was aptly nicknamed--The Beast. The air group had its shakedown on the new HORNET (CV-12), which was also the shakedown for the carrier. Three of the first four Helldivers to launch went into the drink. When they asked me what was wrong they showed me they were using the proper take-off distances that were called for. I explained that those distances were calculated on results obtained by experienced pilots. Our pilots were new, and some had only six or seven hours in the SB2C. They had not taken off from a carrier since their early training days. We backed them up a hundred feet, and it solved that problem.

What about the Avenger?
That was a fine airplane. We never had any trouble with it.

Did you use it in CVG-15 to carry bombs or torpedoes?
The only time I remember using torpedoes was in the Battle of Leyte Gulf on October 25, 1944. We had the better Mark 18 torpedoes by then. The earlier ones just were not any good. Otherwise the Avengers carried bombs.

Did they act as horizontal bombers, or just how did they deliver their bombs?
They used glide bombing, diving at about forty to forty-five degrees. This compares to the Hellcat where we dive bombed at about seventy degrees.

I read somewhere that Hellcat pilots often "dragged" their landing gear, using them as air brakes while dive bombing. Did you ever do that?
No. It may have been done, but I never did it.

When you dive bombed, what bomb did you usually carry?
Most of the time it was a 500-pound bomb, and sometimes a 1000-pounder. On a few occasions I carried two 500-pound bombs. At other times I carried a bomb and rockets. After changing to the F6F-5, I almost always carried rockets.

Carrier Air Group 15 had an outstanding war record. Let's talk about that some. What would you like to say about your Air Group?
During our combat tour, which extended from April until November 1944, our ship was never hit. We never lost a TBF or SB2C we escorted to air-to-air combat. We lost some to anti-aircraft fire, but never to Japanese fighters. We had a total of twenty-seven aces in the group. Of 318 victories by the group, 315 were made by Hellcats. We destroyed 348 aircraft on the ground, not 313 as has been reported before.

Wasn't the ESSEX hit by a suicide pilot in November 1944?
That's right. It was just a week or two after we had left. We went home on the USS BUNKER HILL (CV-17).

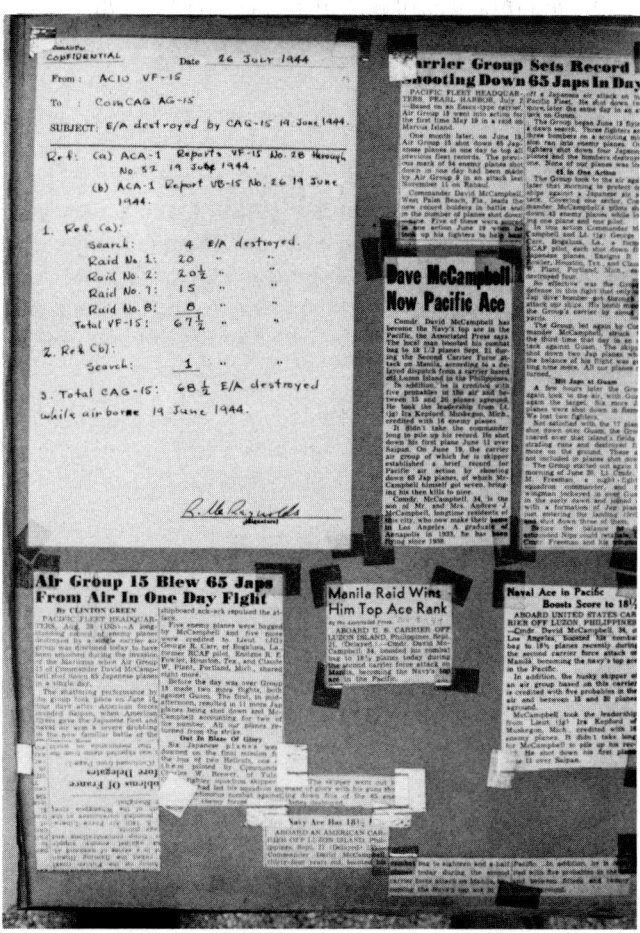

This is a photograph of one of many pages in Captain McCampbell's personal scrapbooks. At the top left is a note to him tallying the kills of CVG-15 to that point in time. (McCampbell)

It is easy to see that you really liked the Hellcat. Did it have any faults as far as you were concerned?
Yes, there was one thing about it I did not like. When the wings were folded there was not enough room between the folded wing and the fuselage to allow a man to easily climb up to the cockpit. Twice, when I had squeezed in between the wing and cockpit, the wings were unlocked and began moving to the extended position. It crushed me against the fuselage. Once it hurt my back, and it continued to bother me for a couple of weeks. Other than that, I have no complaints about the Hellcat.

In turning our attention to your personal experiences, what do you remember about learning to fly?

When I was assigned to VF-4 flying F3Fs, I had to learn to fly on the wing of "Jumpin Joe" Clifton. He had been a fullback on the Navy football team in 1930, and had a tick or jerk of the neck. He would fly with his hands off the controls up on the area above the instrument panel. With his jerk of the head his aircraft would jerk, and it was really something to try to fly formation with him.

I remember that you were an LSO (Landing Signal Officer) early in the war.
Yes, I was an LSO on the RANGER (CV-4) and the WASP (CV-7).

Something that is interesting to me is landing over the bow with the ship steaming astern. Did you ever land aircraft over the bow as an LSO?
I remember doing that on the WASP. Once a pilot was coming in and I gave him a wave-off. When you land over the stern you turn to the left when you take a wave-off, but when landing over the bow you have to turn to the right. Well, this pilot instinctively turned to the left and almost hit the bridge.

I've seen a photograph of the second YORKTOWN (CV-10) recovering aircraft over the bow. Did you ever do it on the ESSEX or any other ESSEX class carrier, or did you ever see it done?
No. I never saw it done on the ESSEX.

You mentioned flying the F3F, and I know you flew the F4F. What other Grumman fighters did you fly?
I flew them all up to the F9F Cougar. After the war I was Coordinator of Tests at Patuxent, and we had all of them there. It gave me an opportunity to fly each of them.

Here Captain McCampbell is shown checking out in the F9F-8T (TF-9J) Cougar. The photograph was taken in 1959 shortly before he took command of the USS BON HOMME RICHARD. (McCampbell)

You always had your own personal aircraft. Was this true for most pilots in your group?
No. I was the only one with my own aircraft. I had the same plane captain the entire time, and the same wingman except for my first two missions. Either I would lead the strike or the fighter squadron commander would. We would seldom be in the air at the same time.

Air Group 15 was obviously very proficient at shooting down enemy aircraft. This brings to mind the division that LT Valencia put together in VF-9. It consisted of the same four pilots that worked together constantly and devised tactics to shoot down enemy aircraft. Did any divisions in Air Group 15 do that?
No. That was a difficult thing to do. Pilots get sick, or cannot fly at times. A pilot needs to be able to perform all missions and fill any slot. Certainly that worked well for Valencia, it was not something that could be done generally. I knew Valencia, and he was a good pilot. I trained him in carrier landings at Melbourne.

Let's move now to your personal experiences. You mentioned earlier that the Japanese aircraft that you shot down usually exploded or caught fire. Did any of the pilots ever get out?
I only saw one parachute, and that was on the Frances I shot down. But it was a crewman, not the pilot. I decided to try my rockets, so I fired them at the plane. It must have scared the crewman, and he jumped. I then shot the aircraft down with my guns.

What was your closest call?
It was on my second mission on the Marcus Island raid. I still had on my external fuel tank, and was hit with what must have been a 40mm shell. It caused a fire that got up into the fuselage and burned out my radios. Wayne Morris (the Hollywood actor who became a Hellcat ace and who was married to McCampbell's niece) **told me about the fire before my radios went out. I lost my left aileron and had to make a flaps-up landing. I also had to use the emergency CO-2 bottles to get my landing gear down. After landing, someone removed the clock from the aircraft, and then it was shoved overboard since it was burned out so bad. From then on I almost always dropped my tank before entering combat. My first wingman, Fred Burnham, was killed over Marcus Island, being shot down by anti-aircraft fire.**

When I heard you speak several years ago, I remember you telling about your landing after the famous flight when you shot down nine aircraft. Would you recount that experience?
That was close too. On my way in I called the ESSEX and told them I was low on gas and needed to get back aboard. They told me that there was no problem and to come on in. When I got there I could see that the flight deck was loaded with aircraft. They asked me to hold for fifteen minutes, but I told them I did not have the fuel for more than ten minutes. So instead I landed aboard the LANGLEY (CVL-27). After being released from the arresting gear, I pushed the throttle to taxi forward, and the engine quit. I was out of gas. You see, when the

aircraft is flying level, it has a few more gallons of usable fuel than it does when it is sitting on its landing gear. I was that low, so once on the carrier the engine quit.

Weren't you out of ammunition too?
Yes. They looked at my guns and told me there were only six rounds left in one of the outboard guns.

Did you ever receive much damage in air-to-air combat?
No. I never got more than just a few holes.

Did you usually launch by flying off the deck or by catapult?
I always launched first, and if it was a big strike they would get as many aircraft up on the flight deck as possible. This did not leave enough room to fly off, so I usually launched by catapult. It was almost always the starboard catapult. Aircraft would continue to launch by catapult until there was enough room for a deck launch. Then the rest would simply fly off.

Can you give a summary of the missions that you flew?
I flew seventy-two missions that included 220 hours, or about three hours per hop. I was involved in combat on sixty-one of the missions. Most of the time was spent attacking targets on the ground, second was attacking ships, and third was air-to-air combat. I would usually lead the air group, and sometimes would be the target coordinator, leading all aircraft from all of the carriers that were involved. I never flew CAP (Combat Air Patrol), and I was only twice involved in scrambles. The first was on June 19th during the "Turkey Shoot" when I shot down seven aircraft on two flights, and then on October 24th when I shot down the nine. The following day I was the target coordinator when we went after and sunk the carriers ZUIKAKU, ZUIHO, CHITOSE, and CHIYODA.

This photograph was taken from an aircraft of CVG-15 on October 25, 1944, during the Battle of Leyte Gulf. It shows the Japanese battleship/seaplane carrier ISE. The ship was later sunk on July 28, 1945. CDR McCampbell led the raid on Ozawa's "decoy" carriers that included the ISE and her sister the HYUGA. (McCampbell)

You shot down thirty-four aircraft in air-to-air combat. How many aircraft did you destroy on the ground?
I claimed twenty-one destroyed on the ground plus eleven probably destroyed.

Roy Rushing was your wingman for all but your first missions over Marcus. How many kills did he get?
Roy shot down thirteen aircraft, mostly Zekes, Hamps, or Oscars. They were all fighters. One time Roy and I were coming back in to land on the ESSEX. We passed over the sinking PRINCETON (CVL-23). The gunners must have been jittery, and the HORNET (CV-12) fired at us with their five-inch guns. We were too high for them to hit us, but the gunnery officer aboard the HORNET was an old friend of mine, and I talked about it to him.

Did you ever lose any aircraft to "friendly" fire?
Not that we know of.

How often did you use the water injection for extra power?
Very seldom. One time I remember is when I used it to get away from my own wingman. After making a pass I saw an aircraft behind me, and I could not tell what it was. Thinking it might be Japanese, I went to emergency power, but the plane stayed with me. Finally, I called over the radio, "Roy, if that is you behind me, rock your wings." He did so, and I knew I was all right. But I almost never used the water injection.

Your famous flight where you shot down nine aircraft has been well documented, and has been published a number of times. There will be a table showing your victories in the book, but now I would like to hear about your aircraft and your personal markings. Most people know about *Minsi III,* and that there were other aircraft named *Minsi.* Were all your aircraft named *Minsi*?
No, my first aircraft, the one in which I got hit over Marcus Island, was named *Monsoon Maiden.* My plane captain, E. E. Caroll, thought that one up, and painted it on both sides of the cockpit.

Are there any photographs of that aircraft with those markings?
No, not that I know of. I don't really remember what the marking looked like.

Your next aircraft was an F6F-3 named *The Minsi.*
Yes. Minsi was the nickname of a girl I knew. Her real name was Mary Blatz.

This is the only known photograph of The Minsi, an F6F-3 which was McCampbell's second Hellcat.
(National Archives)

Minsi II was an F6F-5. It is seen here undergoing maintenance aboard the USS ESSEX while the ship was at an anchorage--probably Ulithi. The device attached in front of the propeller was for boresighting the guns. Careful examination of this photograph will reveal the edges of four kill flags that are mostly hidden by the crewman standing on the wing. The final score for Minsi II was ten and one-half victories. McCampbell got rid of this aircraft after the engine quit on him twice.
(U.S. Navy)

McCampbell is shown here on the left wing of Minsi II, which was his third Hellcat. There are ten and one-half kills, making him a double ace. The rest of the kills would be made in Minsi III. The kills and name Minsi II were on both sides of the aircraft. *(McCampbell)*

A smiling David McCampbell sits in the cockpit of Minsi III near the end of his combat tour. Thirty kill markings are now visible beneath the cockpit. This is the highest number of kills displayed on Minsi III. *(McCampbell)*

I have seen only one photograph of *The Minsi*. It has no kills on it. Did it ever have any kill markings?
No. I did not get any kills in that aircraft.

What color was the name *The Minsi* painted in, and was it on both sides?
I really do not remember what color it was, but it was on both sides of the cockpit. I really don't remember much about that one.

Next came an F6F-5 named *Minsi II*. What about the markings on that aircraft?
There were up to ten and one-half kills on that aircraft, and they were on both sides. So was the name. But the engine on that aircraft cut out on me twice at high altitude. I got it restarted both times, but had to call for an emergency landing. I could not have that. The mechanics could never determine what was wrong with it, so I got rid of it.

Then came *Minsi III*, which was your best known aircraft. I have a color photograph that shows that the name was in yellow. Was it on both sides, and were the kills on both sides? I've never seen an actual photograph of the left side.
Yes, both the name and the kills were on both sides as they had been on *Minsi II*. The kills were stickers rather than being painted on. Also I had "CAG" added in black at some time to the white tail band.

I've seen photos of the aircraft with a varying number of kills. Did it ever carry all thirty-four kills?
No, the most that were on *Minsi III* was thirty. *Minsi IV* was the only one to have thirty-four.

I must admit that I did not know there was a *Minsi IV*. Tell me about that aircraft.
Well, I call it *Minsi IV*. It was a Hellcat given to me when I returned to the States. I flew around to twenty-three

This is the aircraft that Captain McCampbell refers to as Minsi IV. It was the only aircraft to carry all thirty-four kills. Note that the flags are further forward than they were on Minsi III, and that the rays go in the opposite direction. At the time this photograph was taken, the name Minsi III had not been added, but, according to Captain McCampbell, it was added later.
(McCampbell)

Naval Air Stations in a three week period in January 1945. I would show the movie, The Fighting Lady, and then would answer questions. They painted the aircraft with all thirty-four kills, and later put *Minsi III* on it like I had in combat. But to me the aircraft was *Minsi IV*.

You hold the record for the most kills on one mission, and the most for one combat tour. You received the Medal of Honor. What are you the most proud of?
It is the fact that I was never shot down and never bailed out. Many of the top aces cannot say that. I only had minor damage in air-to-air combat.

McCampbell received his Medal of Honor from President Roosevelt in January 1945. *(McCampbell)*

The following is a list of Captain McCampbell's confirmed aerial victories. All dates are in 1944. The list was provided by Captain McCampbell during the interview:

Date	Kills
June 11	1 Zeke
June 13	1 Betty
June 19	5 Judys
	2 Zekes
June 23	1 1/2 Zekes*
September 9	1 Frances
September 12	1 Jack
	2 Zekes
September 13	2 Nates
	1 Oscar
September 22	1 Dinah
September 24	1/2 Pete**
October 21	1 Dinah
	1 Nate
October 24	5 Zekes
	2 Hamps
	2 Oscars
November 5	1 Zeke
	1 Val
November 11	1 Oscar
November 14	1 Oscar

* 1/2 Zeke shared with Claude Plant
** 1/2 Pete shared with Ray Nall

MODELERS SECTION
KIT REVIEWS

OLDER COLLECTABLE KITS

Note: The Hellcat has been well represented over the years by numerous kits in scales ranging from 1/205th to 1/32nd. At least thirty different boxes have been released, but on many occasions the plastic was the same as it had been on an earlier kit. A fair number of molds have been shared around the world. For this reason, only one Hellcat kit is really listed among the highly collectable kits, this being the Frog (Penguin) kit in 1/72nd scale. In the box or built up, it brings $60.00 and up. Jim Galloway, a well known kit collector, has provided the following list and information on the older collectable kits of the Hellcat that are no longer available.

Elvin F6F-5 in 1/205th Scale

Other than being listed in all three kit collector's price guides, there is no other information available on this kit.

UPC F6F-5 in 1/205th Scale

This kit was numbered 8025, and was a re-release of the earlier Elvin kit. It was one of the six "Pee Wees" issued by UPC, and brings from $1.00 to $3.00 today.

Sanwa Tokyo Palmo F6F-5 in 1/119th Scale

The only source listed for this small kit is Carlton Shank's original 1972 issue of "Collectors Guide to Model Aircraft and Rocket/Missile/Space Kits."

Marusan F6F-5 in 1/100th Scale

This kit was released around 1965 and was numbered 465. Today it brings a price of $3.00 to $6.00.

Classic F6F in 1/100th Scale

The only mention of this kit is in Shank's 1972 guide. No other information is available.

Marusan F6F-5 in 1/100th Scale

This kit, numbered 7063, was a re-release of the earlier Marusan 1/100th scale Hellcat mentioned above. It also goes for $3.00 to $6.00 on today's market.

UPC F6F in 1/100th Scale

UPC re-released the earlier Marusan kit under its own label. It is worth about $2.00 to $4.00 today.

Lindberg F6F in 1/96th Scale

This was Lindberg kit number 424. It had a one-piece wing and a pilot's head that was molded into the left fuselage half. It was armed with six rockets and had twenty-one blue pieces and a clear canopy. The main collector's value is in the full color card printed on the back of the box. It is valued today from $3.00 to $6.00.

Hema F6F-5 in 1/96th Scale

This is simply a re-release of the Lindberg kit covered immediately above. It is worth about $5.00 to $9.00 on today's market.

Nitto F6F-5 in 1/77th Scale

This was Nitto kit number 5, and is presently valued in the $3.00 to $6.00 price range.

Frog (Penguin) F6F-3 in 1/72nd Scale

As mentioned above, this is the one truly collectable kit of the Hellcat today. It was numbered 115P, and was released around 1947. All Penguin kits are highly collectable, although many are starting to warp due to chemical reaction. The kits only provided the basic aircraft shape, and had little detail, but they are examples of early injection molding. One in mint condition in the original box would go for around $100.00.

Frog F6F-3 in 1/72nd Scale

This should not be confused with the kit covered immediately above. This is kit number F245G, and is worth from $3.00 to $6.00. It had markings for Number 800 Squadron from the HMS EMPEROR, and Number 1839 Squadron from the HMS INDOMITABLE. It was molded in gray plastic consisting of thirty-six pieces. The landing gear may be displayed either up or down. The cockpit is one piece, consisting of a pilot, seat, and bulkhead. There were no other details to speak of.

Lindberg F6F-5 in 1/72nd Scale

Kit number 484 was released around 1967, and today brings $3.00 to $6.00. It consisted of twenty-four silver pieces and a clear canopy. It had very fine raised rivet and panel line details. There was no interior provided. Decals included four national insignias, an aircraft number of 24 for the fuselage and tail, and seven small kill markings.

Midoro (KSN) F6F-5 in 1/67th Scale

No information is available on this kit except it is listed in the $3.00 to $6.00 price range.

Aurora F6F in 1/51st Scale

Released in 1954, kit number 40-69 is worth from $5.00

to $9.00 today. It had a two-piece clear stand, a clear canopy, and twenty-five dark blue pieces. The wings were solid, and there was very heavy rivet detail. The pilot's head was molded into both sides of the fuselage. "Baby Boomer" modelers will remember this as one original "Famous Fighters" from Aurora.

Aurora F6F in 1/51st Scale

As number 40-79, this was a 1960 re-release of 40-69 above. It is worth $4.00 to $8.00 today.

Lindberg F6F in 1/50th Scale

Kit number 515 was released about 1955, and has a present market value of $3.00 to $6.00. It had thirty-seven medium blue plastic parts to include a two-piece stand. There was also a clear canopy. There were two bombs and a centerline fuel tank to hang under the model. A very crude pilot figure and seat were the only items provided for the interior. Decals included four national insignias, two small U.S. NAVYs, six number 12s in three different sizes, a BuNo of 56874, eight Japanese kill markings, and two blue wing walks.

Lindberg F6F in 1/50th Scale

Kit number 558 was simply a re-release of 515 with British markings. It will go for about $3.00 to $6.00 today.

Lindberg F6F in 1/50th Scale

Kit number 302M was yet another re-release of the original 515. The box art calls this one a "World War II Navy Assault Plane." An electric motor was included to turn the prop. Decals this time had four national insignias, a white fuselage band, four number 32s in white, four letter Vs, and two small number 32s. The BuNo was 56874 as it was in 515. It is worth $6.00 to $10.00 today.

Sanwa Tokyo Palmo F6F-5 in 1/50th Scale

The kit number was 192, and this model is worth $3.00 to $6.00 today. No other information is available on it.

UPC F6F-3 in 1/50th Scale

As if Lindberg had not already released its own kit enough, UPC re-released it again as kit number 6073. Its present market value is $4.00 to $8.00.

Marusan F6F-3 in 1/48th Scale

This unusual kit was molded in clear plastic. It is number 851, and is worth about $6.00 to $10.00 today.

GENERALLY AVAILABLE KITS
1/144th SCALE KITS

AHM F6F-5, Kit Number K-408-79

It may take some looking to find this small kit of the Hellcat, but since this kit, and the one from Revell covered next, are the only two F6Fs ever released in 1/144th scale, we thought it best to provide complete reviews on them. This model has some shape problems, most noticeably the propeller (which is unusable) and the vertical tail. The shape of the tail can be improved with some filing, particularly on the leading edge, but it is impossible to get it entirely correct without rebuilding it completely with plastic card. The last part that is poorly shaped is the external fuel tank, and it should be discarded. If one is desired, it should be built from scratch.

As is the case with most kits which are small, many of the details are missing. There are no rocket rails under the wings, and these were standard on the F6F-5. There is no cockpit at all, and no representation of a pilot. In about ten minutes time we added a cockpit to our model using scrap plastic. This included an instrument panel, consoles, seat, control column, and rear bulkhead. It added a lot to the model even though we positioned the canopy in the closed position. There is no pitot tube, but this could be added with fine wire if desired.

Each main landing gear is molded as one piece, including strut, wheels, and doors all molded together. It is quite fragile, and the wheels and tires are too small in diameter. The ailerons and elevators have too many ribs which are also too pronounced.

If time is taken to reshape the vertical tail and replace the propeller with one that is more accurate, a decent little model of the Hellcat can be constructed from this kit. Fit is generally good, with only a little filling and sanding required.

This AHM kit in 1/144th scale was built as an F6F-5 from VF-29 and the USS CABOT. The quarter gives a size comparison for this tiny model.

Revell F6F-3, Kit Number H-1024

This kit has been released several times by Revell USA and Revell of England. It is now hard to find, and we would like to see Revell reissue the kit again. It is definitely the better of the two Hellcat models in 1/144th scale, and could easily be modified from an F6F-3 to an F6F-5.

65

The model is much better shaped than the AHM kit with the propeller, vertical tail, and external fuel tank all correctly represented. Small braces will have to be added to the fuel tank, but it is at least correctly shaped. The radio mast angles forward as it did on early F6F-3s, and this may have to be changed depending on the particular aircraft that is being modeled.

The kit is molded in light gray plastic and has finely detailed raised surface scribing. Control surfaces and the wing fold line are recessed. The engine is molded into the cowling and looks quite acceptable for this small scale. Again, each main landing gear is all one piece, and the wheels and tires are the correct diameter. The main door is a little heavy and may benefit from some filing down. However, care should be taken if this is done, since the part is fragile enough as it is. A two-piece clear stand is provided, as is a clear canopy which includes windscreen, sliding portion, and small rear windows all in one piece. There is no cockpit at all, but the basics could quickly be added from scrap plastic. The only important detail problem with the kit is that the guns are not represented. They can easily be added from stretched sprue or very fine wire.

Of all the kits that are being reviewed in this section, this is the only one we were not able to build, so comments about the fit cannot be made. But it looks like this kit would build up into an excellent little model, and we recommend it as the better of the 1/144th scale Hellcats. The only problem the modeler will have with it is finding one! Our review model was provided on loan by Jim Galloway.

1/72nd SCALE KITS

Airfix F6F-3 or -5, Kit Number 9 02023

As one of the older Hellcat kits that are still available, this model in not up to today's state-of-the-art in molding and detailing. There are a lot of parts, and they are covered with extensive rivet detail that should be sanded off. The cowl flaps are molded in the open position, and they do not look correct. We recommend sanding them off and rescribing them in the closed position. The more diligent modeler could replace them in the open position with new ones made from plastic card. There are some other shape problems, and it seems that neither the fuselage, wings, or tail sections are quite right.

The model can be built as either a -3 or a -5. Two cowls are provided for this purpose, and for most -5s, the rear windows are simply filled in. Six rockets are included for the -5 version, and two bombs and an external fuel tank complete the external stores. Neither the rockets, bombs, or tank are very well done.

The cockpit is sparse, consisting of a bulkhead and a fair seat. Most modelers will want to add some detailing here. A gunsight should be added, since it will be visible even with the canopy in the closed position.

The main landing gear has some shape problems. Most noticeable is that the main landing gear wells are circular, and this is incorrect. A little work with a sharp knife will correct this. The wings can be built in the folded or extended position, and this causes a problem no

The Airfix F6F-3 in 1/72nd scale is an older kit with a lot of parts. It is not as good as the more recent releases.

matter which choice is made. If extended, the fit at the fold is bad and will take a lot of fitting, filling, and sanding to get it right. If built in the folded position, the insides of the wings are visible, and this is very phoney looking. The wing joint detail would have to be added from scratch to make this feature look like a model instead of a toy.

There are some missing details as well. There is no representation of the large hinges for the ailerons. As with almost all kits, the rockets and their launch stubs are molded together, and for mold release considerations, the rockets are positioned so that their fins make a + instead of an X when viewed from behind.

Considering its age, this kit is not all that bad, but when comparing it to the newer 1/72nd scale kits, it leaves a lot to be desired.

Fujimi F6F-5, Kit Number A 12-100

This is an older Fujimi release, and it is nowhere near as good as Fujimi's more recent kits such as their A-4 and F-4 models.

Actually, this kit is marked as 1/70th scale, but it fits closely in a 1/72nd scale collection. Actual measurements show it a bit larger than a correct 1/72nd scale, but it is not really 1/70th scale either. Like the Airfix kit, it has some shape problems, most noticeable of which is the vertical tail which is totally incorrect. It is too deep in chord, and a lot of plastic will have to be removed from the leading edge. Further, the leading edge is too vertical and needs to be angled back more. Some filing and sanding can bring this to a decent shape, but it would be quite difficult to get it really correct. The vertical tail also appears to be too thick, and this would be even more difficult to correct.

A lot of detailing is missing or is incorrect. For example, there are no links on the landing gear, and although the model represents a -5, the radio mast angles forward as it did on early -3s. This is easily corrected, however. The engine is molded as one piece with no real detail other than the cylinders. The pitot is on the wrong wing, the landing gear is flimsy, and it has a poor fit. The guns are poor, with the center and outboard guns being the same length. The aileron hinges are two small, the gun ejector slots are too long, there is no gunsight, and the cockpit is sparse. The canopy is wrong, being the design used on the F6F-3, and what's worse, the sliding portion has too much of a bubble at the forward end.

This is a very critical review, but the kit does have these problems. It simply cannot be recommended for the serious scale modeler.

Heller F6F-5, Kit Number 155

(See Testors review below.)

Matchbox F6F-3, Kit Number PK-18

This is one of the Matchbox kits that is molded in wild colors with trench-like scribing. Pea green and olive were the colors chosen for this kit, and the box art shows a green Hellcat taking off from a carrier that is supposed to be the USS YORKTOWN (CV-10). The fit is poor, and so is the detailing. The worst point here is that the top and bottom halves of each wing do not meet at the tips as would be expected. Instead, the most outboard panels of the upper wings are molded into the lower wing pieces. The fit between the two is not good at all, and this makes for a bad joint right on top of the wing.

The cockpit does not even have a representation for a decent seat or bulkhead. Much work will be required here if satisfactory results are to be obtained. At least there is a gunsight, and this is something that is missing from some of the other kits. The engine detail is also lacking, with only the cylinders being represented. All of the details for the forward portion of the engine are missing.

The landing gear is provided twice; once for a gear-down, and once for a gear-up configuration. In either case, the detail and accuracy are poor. The main gear is flimsy, and the links are too big. Surface scribing is minimal when it comes to detail, and what is there is way too deep. It provides evidence that engraved scribing is not worth much if it is executed poorly.

The shape of the vertical tail is wrong, but it is not as bad as it is on the Fujimi kit. Other shape problems exist, and it would take a lot of time and effort to work them out. Although the kit represents an F6F-3, the lateral exhaust fairing (present on most F6F-3s) is missing. The external fuel tank is fair, but the braces for it are missing. The aileron hinges are too small, and the one-piece canopy is thick and does not fit well around the rear windows.

With much better models of the Hellcat available in 1/72nd scale, this kit is best left to the collectors. It is not one that should be considered by serious modelers.

Hasegawa Hellcats, Various Kit Numbers and Versions

Hasegawa first released a Hellcat in 1/72nd scale as Kit Number 1165. It has been released a number of times since, and it is possible to build either an F6F-3 or F6F-5 from any of these releases. More recently, Hasegawa has reworked the kit and has released F6F-5E and F6F-5N night-fighting Hellcat kits. The night fighter kits are the same kit as released earlier with the extra parts required for the night fighter also provided. These include the radar pod, cannon armament, exhaust flash suppressors (for use on the F6F-5N only) and even different instrument panels with the radar scope included. Otherwise these kits are all the same, and the following comments apply to each of them.

The kit builds into a -3 easier than it does a -5, since no rocket stubs are provided for the -5 versions. These will have to be added from card stock for any basic -5 or the -5E and -5N night fighters. Two canopies are provided, one for the -3 and the other for the -5 variants. But in each case the windscreen and the sliding part are molded as a single piece, so displaying the model with an open canopy cannot be accomplished unless a new canopy is vacu-formed. A commercial vacu-formed canopy is available from Squadron, and this will also solve this problem effectively. The area where the rear windows go in an F6F-3 or an early F6F-5 is solid plastic, but it is thinner than the rest of the fuselage. All the modeler has to do is open these up and insert the clear pieces if these windows are appropriate for the aircraft he is modeling.

The cockpit has some detail, but decals are used to represent the instruments and controls. There are some errors in the cockpit. Most notably, the instrument panel is molded with a center console that comes all the way down to the floor. This does not exist on the real aircraft. Instead, there should be a pedestal that is situated several inches further forward than the instrument panel as illustrated on pages 38 and 39. In addition, this pedestal does not come up as high as the lower edge of the instrument panel. There are two side consoles represented, but the left side is not actually a console in the real aircraft.

The main wheel wells are fully enclosed, but they are too shallow and the detailing is incorrect. There is a good external fuel tank that includes the main braces, but the small forward braces will have to be added. Optional parts allow the modeler to choose between the angled and vertical radio masts as appropiate. The engine is well represented, and the raised scribing is well executed,

Hasegawa's Hellcat kits in 1/72nd scale are quite good. The basic kit can be built as an F6F-3 or an F6F-5, and F6F-3E and F6F-5N kits have also been released. The author built this one in Alexander Vraciu's markings.

being both delicate and accurate. The landing gear is nicely detailed, and it is sturdy enough to support the model.

In kit number 617, decals are provided for three aircraft. These include Varaciu's number 19 from the USS INTREPID, *The Minsi*, which was McCampbell's second Hellcat after *Monsoon Maiden*, and *Minsi III*. The problem is that for *Minsi III*, only the markings for the right side are included. The markings were on both sides of the aircraft, and using the decals from two kits won't help. This is because the yellow *Minsi III* should be angled back in the other direction on the right side. Markings for this aircraft have been on decal sheets many times, but not once have they been done correctly.

The problems that exist with this Hasegawa model are relatively small, and we recommend it as one of the better Hellcat kits in 1/72nd scale.

Academy/Minicraft F6F-3/-5, Kit Number 2121

This is an excellent 1/72nd scale model, and overall we would rate it as better than the Hasegawa 1/72nd scale Hellcats. Each has some specific features that are better than the other, but many modelers will choose this kit simply because it has recessed panel lines. Also in this kit's favor is that rockets are provided. Therefore, building an F6F-5 is much easier than using the Hasegawa kits which have no rockets or stubs. The rockets have correctly shaped stubs molded with them, and the aft ends with the fins are separate pieces. This means they may be glued in place with the fins in the correct X configuration. The rockets are fitted with the larger warheads, and while this was not the most common type used on the Hellcat, they are correct. If an F6F-3 is to be built, the holes for the rocket stubs in the underside of the wings must be filled in and sanded.

Two bombs are also provided as under-wing ordnance, and the appropriate bomb racks are included. The instructions for gluing the bomb racks in place are backward. Mount the racks in the opposite direction than what is shown on the instruction sheet.

There is a centerline fuel tank included, and it has a rib running all the way around it laterally. These tanks were made by various manufacturers, and there were some minor differences between them. We have seen a few photographs with this rib running laterally instead of vertically, so tanks like this did exist. But most did not have the lateral ribbing. It should be easy to remove if desired.

The engine is better than most found in 1/72nd scale kits, with the forward row of cylinders and crankcase being a separate piece. However, some of the smaller accessories are missing from the crankcase. The landing gear is well executed, although the main gear wells could use a little detailing. For example, they are not completely enclosed as they should be. A little plastic card should cure this problem very easily. But the main wheel wells are deeper than those in the Hasegawa kits, and this helps make them look more realsitic. The tail wheel has the pneumatic tire as used mainly on land, but it would be rather simple to sand its edges flat to represent the hard rubber tire usually seen on carriers.

The cockpit is better than that in the Hasegawa kit,

Jim Roeder used the Academy/Minicraft 1/72nd scale Hellcat to build this F6F-5 from VF-16 aboard the USS RANDOLPH. (Roeder)

but it is still a bit of a disappointment. There are parts for each side of the cockpit, but they are not accurate or well detailed. There is not even a throttle quadrant. The instrument panel has a center console attached rather than the correct pedestal. Details on the instrument panel and what is supposed to be the center pedestal are provided in the form of a single decal. This has a black background, but the center pedestal should be chromate green. These parts may suffice if the canopy is built closed, but if the cockpit is going to be displayed open, some detailing and correcting will be required.

Windscreens for both the F6F-3 and F6F-5 are provided, and the sliding part of the canopy is a separate piece. This might lead one to believe that it can be displayed in the open position, but this is not the case. It just won't fit down over the spine of the fuselage. A vacu-formed canopy from Squadron will solve the problem and make it easy to display the canopy in the open position.

Most of the detailing on the model itself looks good, but there are a few places that need improvement. First, the hinges on the ailerons are too small, and it would be best to replace them with new ones made from plastic card. The small blue lights on the top of the wings just forward of the ailerons are located too far outboard. Simply fill them in, sand smooth, then rescribe them in the correct locations as shown on page 12 of this book. The forward edge on the tip of the vertical tail is too rounded. Compare it to the drawings in this book and use some plastic card to reshape it.

Although the kit includes all the necessary options to build either an F6F-3 or a -5, the only decals provided are for an F6F-5 from VF-17 aboard the USS HORNET in March 1945.

For the super detailer, Verlinden Productions makes a detailing set for this kit. It has the more common centerline tank without the lateral rib, a new front engine piece, canopy framing, and many cockpit details. Parts are also included to open and detail the left gun compartment.

One plastic part also corrects the shape of the tip of the vertical tail, while other parts in plastic are included for the throttle, gunsight, seat, and bomb racks. Etched metal parts are provided for the instrument panel, side consoles, engine wires, anti-sway braces on the bomb rack, and details for the landing gear. The interior of the gun bay is made from metal parts, but the guns are plastic. This is an expensive set, but it can truly enhance this model and turn it into a masterpiece if the modeler is willing to put in the effort.

With or without the detailing set, this is an excellent kit, and we recommend it as the best Hellcat in 1/72nd scale. One of its other features that we really like is its price, which is about half that of the Hasegawa 1/72nd scale Hellcats.

Testors F6F-5, Kit Number 416

This kit is another example of Testors using someone else's molds and putting the model in their box with new decals. This time the kit is the older Heller F6F-5, and unfortunately, simply reboxing a kit does not correct its problems. This particular kit has some real shortcomings, but there are some good points as well. The old Heller instructions had a very poor exploded view instead of step-by-step instructions, and we cannot understand why Testors retained this exploded view on their instructions rather than improving on it.

The kit is molded in light gray plastic, and no changes were noticed from the original Heller release. Scribing is acceptable, and the engine looks good on the finished model. The canopy is excellent, being the proper one for the -5, and it comes in two pieces. The gun slots under the wings are open as is the area under the cowl flaps. This adds to the appearance of the model.

On the minus side, the rocket stubs are too wide and should be replaced. They are also positioned too far inboard. A check of the drawings in this book will show the correct location. Since the rockets themselves are separate pieces, they can be glued in place with the proper X configuration for the fins instead of the incorrect + position seen on most kits. There are no aileron hinges and no representation of the tail hook. A fuel tank is provided, but its shape is very bad, and we recommend not using it.

The cockpit comes in the form of a tub, and it includes small consoles, a control column, gunsight, and a seat. Most modelers will probably want to do some correcting and detailing here.

Fit is very poor and is made worse by the lack of line-up pins on the wings. The biggest problems come at the point where the wings join the fuselage at the wing root and under the aircraft where the fuselage portion of the wing meets the aft fuselage. Complicating the poor fit is the thin plastic at this point which makes filling and sanding difficult. This wing-fuselage fit problem is due to poor kit design, and it takes care and patience to work out.

Surprisingly, Testors chose decal subjects that were already available from other sources. Carl Brown's *PAPER DOLL* was formerly done by Microscale/Superscale and ESCI. *Minsi III* has previously been done several times. If Testors had corrected the previous mistakes, this would have been understandable, but as has been the case before, the markings for *Minsi III* are provided for only one side of the aircraft. Further, *Minsi III* had the small windows behind the cockpit which this model does not have. So unless the modeler makes this change himself, *Minsi III* cannot be built from this kit anyway. With all of the markings carried by Hellcats that have never been made available to the modeler, it would seem that Testors could have chosen one or more of these instead of picking two that had been done before. By providing new choices, they would have increased the value of their kit. In fairness, it should be noted that Testors is not the only kit manufacturer to include previously available decals in their new releases. We believe that, unless the manufacturer is correcting an error (or errors) in the existing decals, a new choice of decals should be offered. Many modelers might buy the kit just to get the decals.

1/48th SCALE KITS

Fujimi F6F-5, Kit Number 5A4,450

On the box art, this kit is said to be 1/50th scale, and its dimensions are a bit smaller than the standard 1/48th scale. However, it is close enough to be included among the 1/48th scale kit reviews. It is off in several dimensions, with the vertical tail being noticeably too small and incorrect in shape. The box also shows an F6F-3, but the kit inside is of an F6F-5. Markings are for a -3, and the canopy is the type used on the F6F-3, not the -5 that the rest of the kit represents.

The parts are molded in medium blue plastic, and fit is rather poor. The worst area is where the wings join the fuselage. Much rework and plastic surgery is needed to get the wings to mate with the fuselage. Once this is done, a lot of filling and sanding is necessary for the remaining gaps.

The engine lacks detail, and it is molded into the forward cowling piece. Its simplicity is to allow for an electric motor to be installed to turn the propeller. Details are also missing on the landing gear to include the links at

Testors re-released the Heller F6F-5 kit in 1/72nd scale. It was used to build this model of ENS A. R. Ives' Hellcat that caught fire when landing aboard the USS LEXINGTON on February 25, 1945. The markings are those of VF-20.

This is the Fujimi 1/50th scale F6F-5. The markings are those of the Hellcat assigned to LCDR F. A. Bardshar, the CAG of CVG-27 aboard the USS PRINCETON. This aircraft was on the flight deck when the PRINCETON was hit by a bomb from a single Judy, and it was lost when the ship went down.

the oleos. The wheels are made so that they can roll, and any such working parts always detract from the detail and accuracy of a model. The radio mast is angled forward, and this much be changed to the upright position that was used on the F6F-5.

A fair fuel tank that lacks braces, two bombs that are identical to Monogram's, and six rockets are provided to be hung under the model. The rocket stubs are simply round pins rather than having the correct airfoil shape. The rockets are again mounted with the fins in the + configuration rather than the X that they should be.

The cockpit can be built two different ways depending on whether or not the electric motor is installed. Either way, there is no detail at all except for a seat. This is inexcusable for a kit of this size, and some detailing will be required even if the canopy is shown in the closed position.

Monogram F6F-5, Kit Number 5832

When this kit was released, having working parts was an important feature for models. Monogram loaded its Hellcat with lots of them, to include folding wings and retracting landing gear. Naturally, the prop turns, the wheels roll, and the tail hook extends. But these working parts detract from the accuracy and detailing of a kit which is far more important to modelers today. To get the landing gear to retract, Monogram had to make the wings too thick and the wheels too thin. Much of the detail of the landing gear had to be compromised. The folding wings added to the problems. When the wings are folded, you can see through the wing center section, and down into the outer sections. When extended, the fit is not good, and as a result, the model looks more like a toy than a true scale model. But the outline and general shape of the kit is not too bad when working parts do not interfere.

There is no cockpit. Only a rear bulkhead is provided

with a pilot figure that attaches to it. There isn't even a gunsight, and it would be very noticeable in this scale. The canopy is wrong, being of the type used on the F6F-3, but this is fairly easily remedied. We took the time to detail the cockpit, and this added a lot to the model. The engine is molded into the forward cowl piece and lacks any detail other than the cylinders. For the underside, two bombs, six rockets, and a centerline fuel tank with no braces are provided. The rockets are molded with their launch stubs again, and are configured in the incorrect + position instead of the correct X. The stubs do not resemble the real thing. If the rockets are to be used, cut off the stubs, make new ones from plastic card, then add the rockets to the new stubs being sure to attach them so that the fins form an X.

Monogram's old F6F-5 was used to build this model of a Hellcat from VF-17 and the USS HORNET in March 1945.

As has been the case with some of the models we have already covered, the radio mast angles forward, and since this is a -5, it will have to be straightened. Another correction that is required is the relocating of the pitot tube from the left to the right wing where it belongs. The gun ejector slots under the wing are much too long, but these can be shorted rather easily if desired.

This kit is better than the Fujimi kit, which was the only other F6F-5 kit available in anything close to 1/48th scale for many years. But now a much better -5 is obtainable from Hasegawa.

Otaki/Arii F6F-3, Kit Number 2-29 (Otaki) and 0330 (Arii)

Released first by Otaki, then by Arii, this is an excellent model of an F6F-3. It can also be modified fairly easily to a -5 if desired.

The kit is molded in light gray plastic, and the raised panel lines are both fine and accurate. The fairing over the lateral exhaust is not solid as it is on some other kits. It is open, and the exhaust pipes can be seen under it. The wheel wells are enclosed, and although some detailing is present, more could be added. Although the engine is molded into the cowl, it looks good when finished, and the accessories at the front end of the engine are nicely represented. These add to the realism of the engine when the model is completed.

Otaki's excellent 1/48th scale F6F-3 is shown here. The markings are from VF-16 and the USS LEXINGTON for the Wake Island raid in October 1943.

Some cockpit detailing is provided, but it is not really accurate. Additional work is required to make the cockpit more realistic and accurate. The seat is nice and has the belts scribed into it. An instrument panel, gunsight, and rudder pedals are provided. Much of the required work will have to be done to the instrument panel and to the consoles.

The external fuel tank is accurate and includes the larger braces. The smaller forward braces are missing and must be added by the modeler. Two bombs are also provided, but there are no rockets, since these were not carried on the -3 version as a general rule.

One shortcoming is the one-piece canopy. It would have been much better if a two-piece canopy had been provided that could be displayed in the open position. To have an open canopy, the modeler will have to vacu-form the sliding part of the canopy so that it will fit over the fuselage and rear windows. But on the plus side, the bullet-resistant glass is a separate piece under the windscreen as it was on the F6F-3. Wheel chocks and good decals add to the appeal of this kit.

To build an F6F-5, the rear windows would have to be sealed off (except on early -5s). The lateral exhaust fairings must be removed, and the resulting hole most be filled and sanded. Stubs for the rockets must be added, and the canopy will have to be modified. All of this is rather simple and well within the abilities of most modelers.

Hasegawa F6F-3 and F6F-5 Hellcat Kits

This kit was released first as an F6F-3, then as an F6F-5 in the summer of 1996. Both kits are basically the same, with the F6F-5 kit providing a new canopy, rockets, and fairings that go under the fuselage at the wing root. Instructions for the -5 also direct the modeler to fill in some panel lines on the cowling and under the wing. Surprisingly, neither version provides any bombs or bomb racks.

The centerline fuel tank is included, and it is the most accurate one in any Hellcat kit. All of the straps and braces are represented nicely. In almost every respect, the kit is excellent, with good attention to detail throughout. A decal is even included for the Pratt & Whitney logo on the crankcase of the engine.

The cockpit is one of the best we have seen in a 1/48th scale plastic model. Even the pedestal just forward of the instrument panel is basically correct. But it is molded as part of the instrument panel which it shouldn't be. Simply cut it away from the panel, shorten it slightly, and mount it to the cockpit floor just a little forward of the lower edge of the instrument panel. The instrument panel itself has the auxiliary panels which are angled correctly. The seat has the belts and harnesses molded on it. Not all cockpit details are represented, but this is about as good as it gets in a 1/48th scale plastic kit. Without scratchbuilding, the only way to improve on it is to use the resin cockpit from True Details that was designed for this model.

Landing gear detail is also well executed, and while the tires are not weighted, it should be noted that the tires on carrier aircraft were inflated to very high pressures. There were no bulges in them, and the flat spot on the underside was minimal. This could be added to the main tires simply by filing a small flat spot on each. Inside the main gear wells, the prominent hooks which lock the landing gear in the retracted position are missing, and these should be made from plastic card and added. They are quite noticeable. See pages 8 and 9 in this book for a look at these hooks. The tire on the tail wheel is the hard rubber type used on carriers.

In the F6F-3 kit, the windscreen has a separate bullet-resistant glass that fits inside of it as was the case on the actual aircraft. The sliding part of the canopy is marginally too large to be displayed in the open position. This means one will have to be vacu-formed if it is to be built in the open position to show the cockpit detailing. This seems to be a problem with most of the Hasegawa kits coming out, since this is not the only one with a canopy that cannot be built in the open position. Considering the very high price of this kit, a modeler should reasonably expect to have a canopy that could be built open or closed even if two different parts had to be included to do so.

For the -3 variant, the modeler has to open up the windows behind the cockpit. Be very careful doing this, because it is very easy to cut through the forward frame of these windows.

Hasegawa also designed the kit so that the flaps were

Dave Pluth of Chaska, Minnesota, used the Hasegawa 1/48th scale F6F-3 kit to build this tri-colored Hellcat from VF-9 and the USS ESSEX. The decals are from Aeromaster sheet number 48-069. (Pluth)

molded as part of the wings. Again, considering the price of the kit, it would not be unreasonable to expect these to be separate pieces. The flaps were often in the lowered position when the aircraft was on the ground or aboard ship. Hasegawa also represented the gunsight and its access panel on the leading edges of both wings at the root. It should only be on the left wing. Fill in the hole and the panel lines on the right wing and sand smooth.

The landing and taxi light on the leading edge of the left wing is represented only by scribed lines. Suprisingly, there is no clear piece for the lens. We recommend opening up the hole for the light and adding a small piece of clear plastic to make the lens cover. It can be sanded to shape after the wing is assembled, then polish it to remove any scratchces.

An interesting note that shows a lack of effective research on Hasegawa's part is that a clear landing light is provided to go under the left wing. And, as mentioned above, the landing and taxi light on the leading edge of the same wing is represented by scribed lines. Both lights should not be present on the same aircraft. The light under the left wing was on only the first 272 F6F-3s. It was deleted from all Hellcats after F6F-3, BuNo. 08885, so it was not present on almost all aircraft. But ironically, Hasegawa did not include the gun fairings, and these were on the first 900 Hellcats built extending through BuNo. 26195. So any Hellcat with the landing light under the wing would also have had these fairings. (See page 5.) Further, Hasegawa shows the radio antenna in the vertical position, but it was angled forward on the first 909 F6F-3s. It was located just to the right of centerline on the first 2560 F6F-3s, and then just to the left of centerline beginning with BuNo. 41295. Hasegawa did include scribing to represent the lower cowl flap, and this was only on the first 1264 F6F-3s. It was deleted beginning with BuNo. 39999. All of these points are small, and can easily be corrected by the modeler with the possible exception of the gun fairings. We provide this information not to be overly critical, but so a modeler may take the necessary steps to change any of these features as necessary depending on the particular Hellcat he is building.

This is the best Hellcat kit on the market. It is state-of-the art with excellent recessed panel lines and very good fit. Even built straight from the box, it will produce an excellent model. With a little attention to the details discussed in the paragraph immediately above, and with some minor corrections and additions, a modeler can turn this into a real masterpiece. We highly recommend it.

Dave Pluth contributed to this review.

1/32nd SCALE KITS

Hasegawa F6F-3, -5, -5E, -5N, Various Kit Numbers

Hasegawa first released a basic Hellcat kit in 1/32nd scale during the 1970-71 time frame. It could be built as either an F6F-3 or and F6F-5, and it had all of the necessary options to build either version. The model has stood the test of time, and twenty-five years after the initial release, it is still a very fine kit. As they did with their 1/72nd scale Hellcat kits, Hasegawa provided extra parts

The original issue of the large 1/32nd scale Hasegawa Hellcat can be built as either an F6F-3 or an F6F-5. Two subsequent releases provide parts for F6F-3E and F6F-5N night fighters. This model was built by Don Harris of IPMS Atlanta shortly after the kit was originally released in 1971.

and reissued this kit twice as different Hellcat night fighters. The first re-release was of the F6F-5N and the second was of the F6F-5E.

Both gun compartments can be displayed in the open position, and here again, the appearance of the model can be enhanced with some extra detailing. For the F6F-5N, we recommend building the gun bays closed, because Hasegawa did not provide the aft end of two 20-mm cannons to go inside the bays. They did provide the longer and larger barrels that are to be glued to the leading edge of the wing, but the inboard gun inside each bay still remains a .50-caliber machine gun. The instructions for this particular release also show the bays being built only in the closed position.

The engine is a model itself, with each cylinder being an individual part. It looks good when finished, but most modelers will want to take a little time to add wires, drill out exhausts, and add other details. We have seen one of these engines fully detailed, and it looked truly amazing. An excellent fuel tank is provided as are six rockets and stubs for the F6F-5 versions. There is an optional position tail hook, optional position cowl flaps, and an optional lateral exhaust faring depending on what version is being built. The flaps can be assembled in the lowered position, and this improves the appearance and realism of the model. Optional tires are also provided, being included as both plastic and rubber parts. We recommend using the plastic ones.

The wheel wells are nice, but they could be further detailed to include the lock-up hook and other details. The landing gear is nicely done and looks like the real thing.

On the minus side, there are some mold sink holes in the tips of the elevators and the top of the rudder. These should be filled in and sanded smooth. Otherwise the molding and scribing is excellent, and the fit is generally good throughout. The model is rather expensive, and it requires a lot of time to build correctly. Any modeler who starts to build it should be ready to allow a lot of time and put forth considerable care and effort in order to finish with a model that is worthy of a kit of this size and cost. It is an excellent kit, and we recommend it.